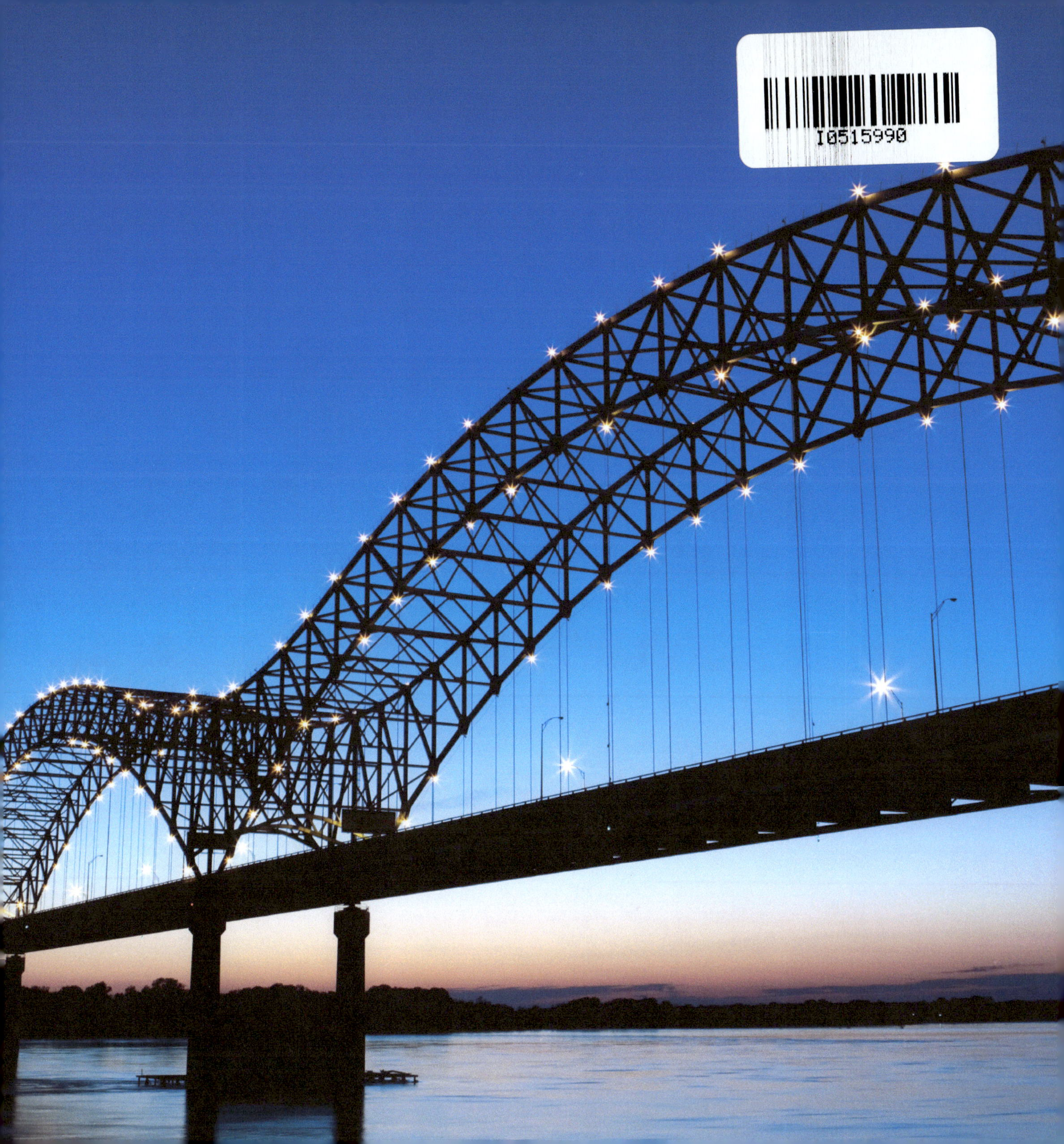

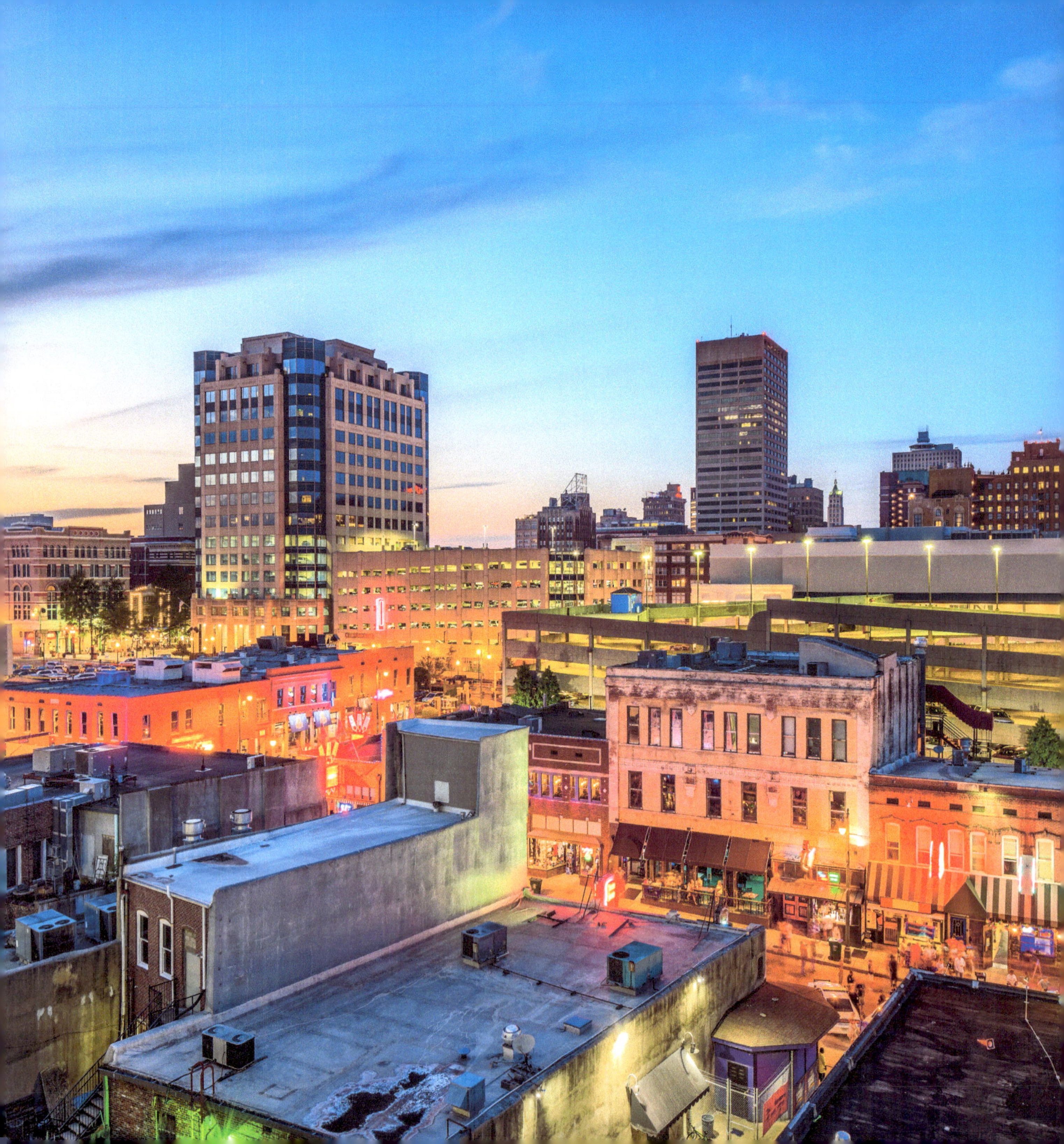

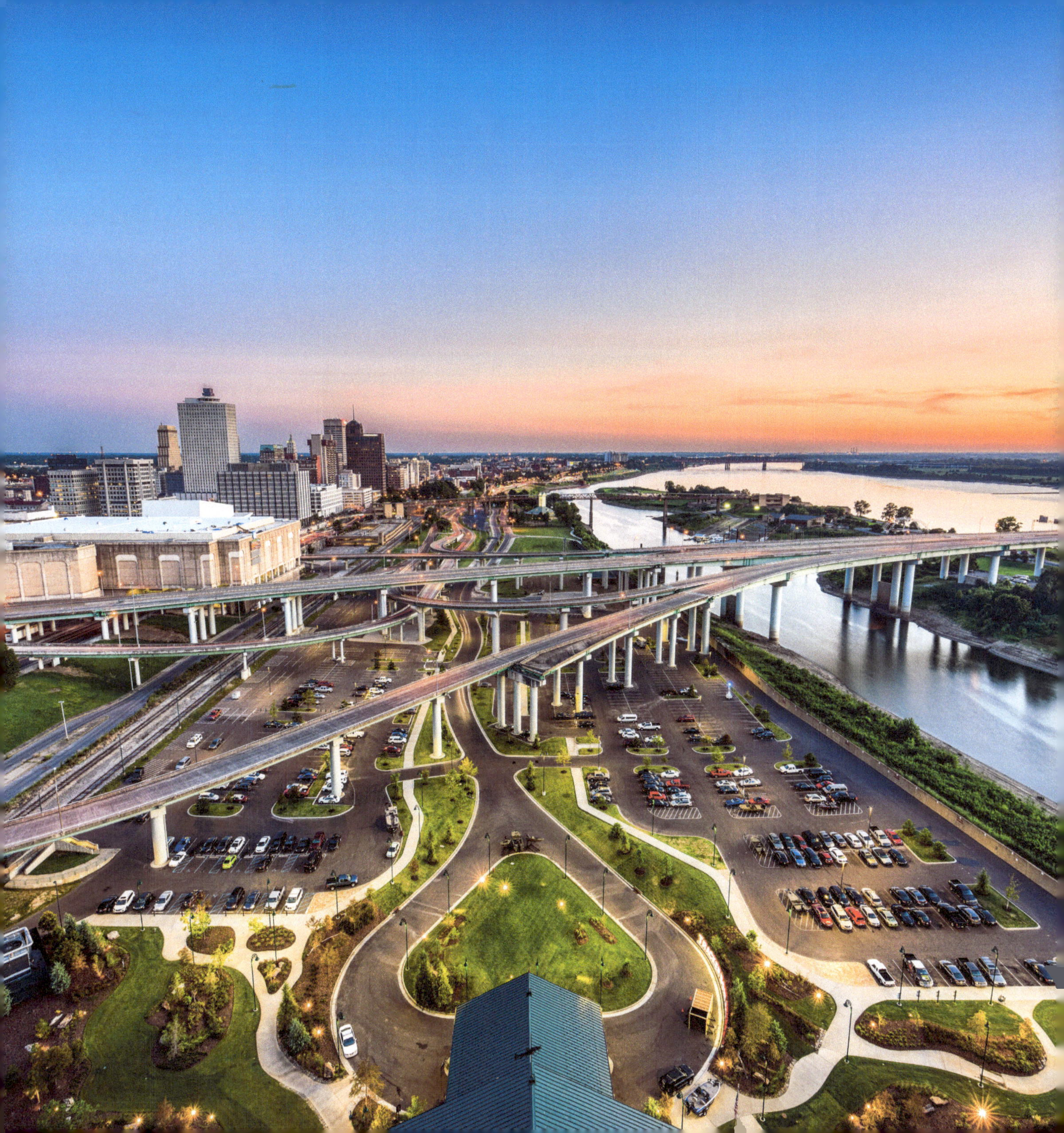

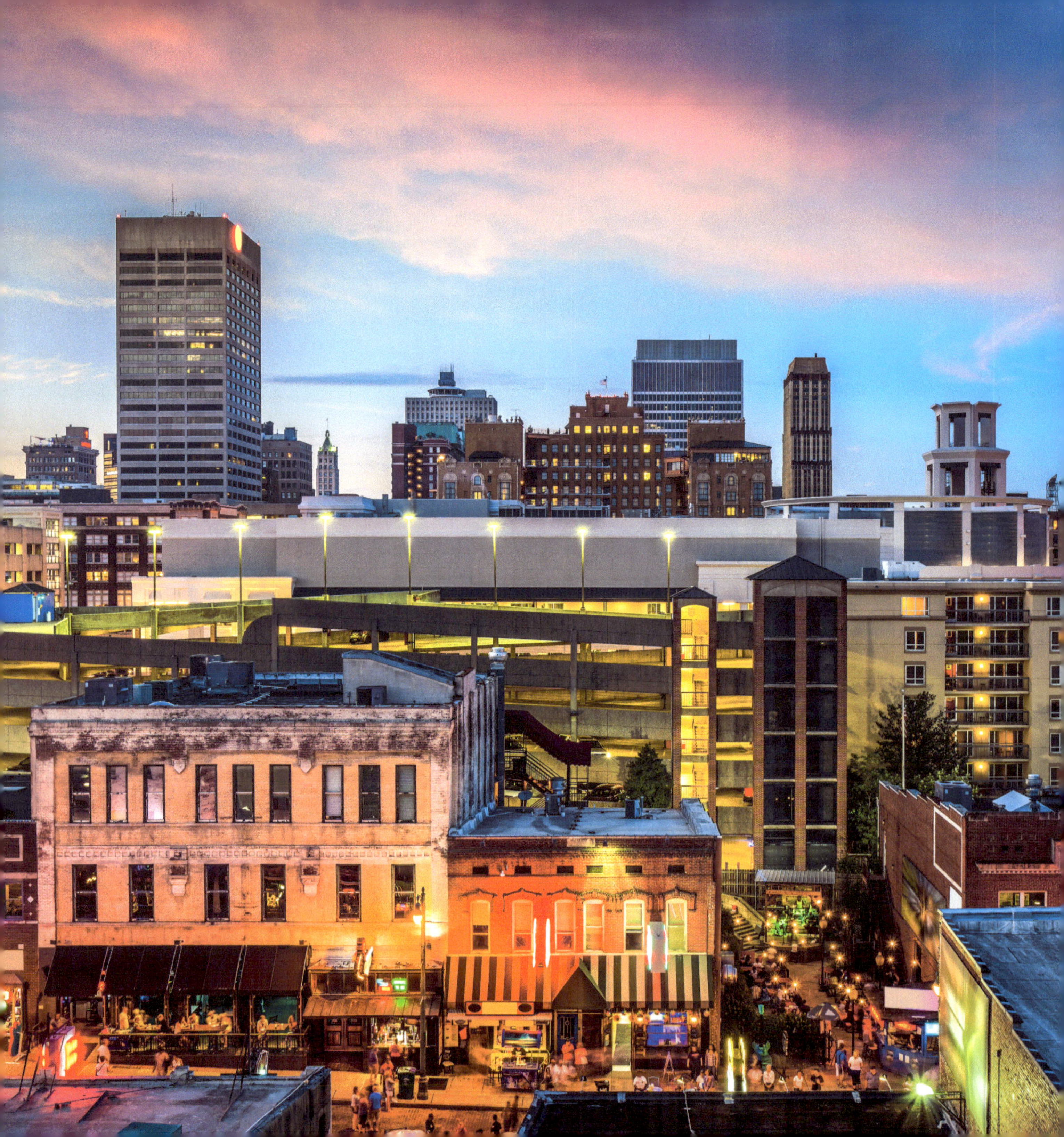

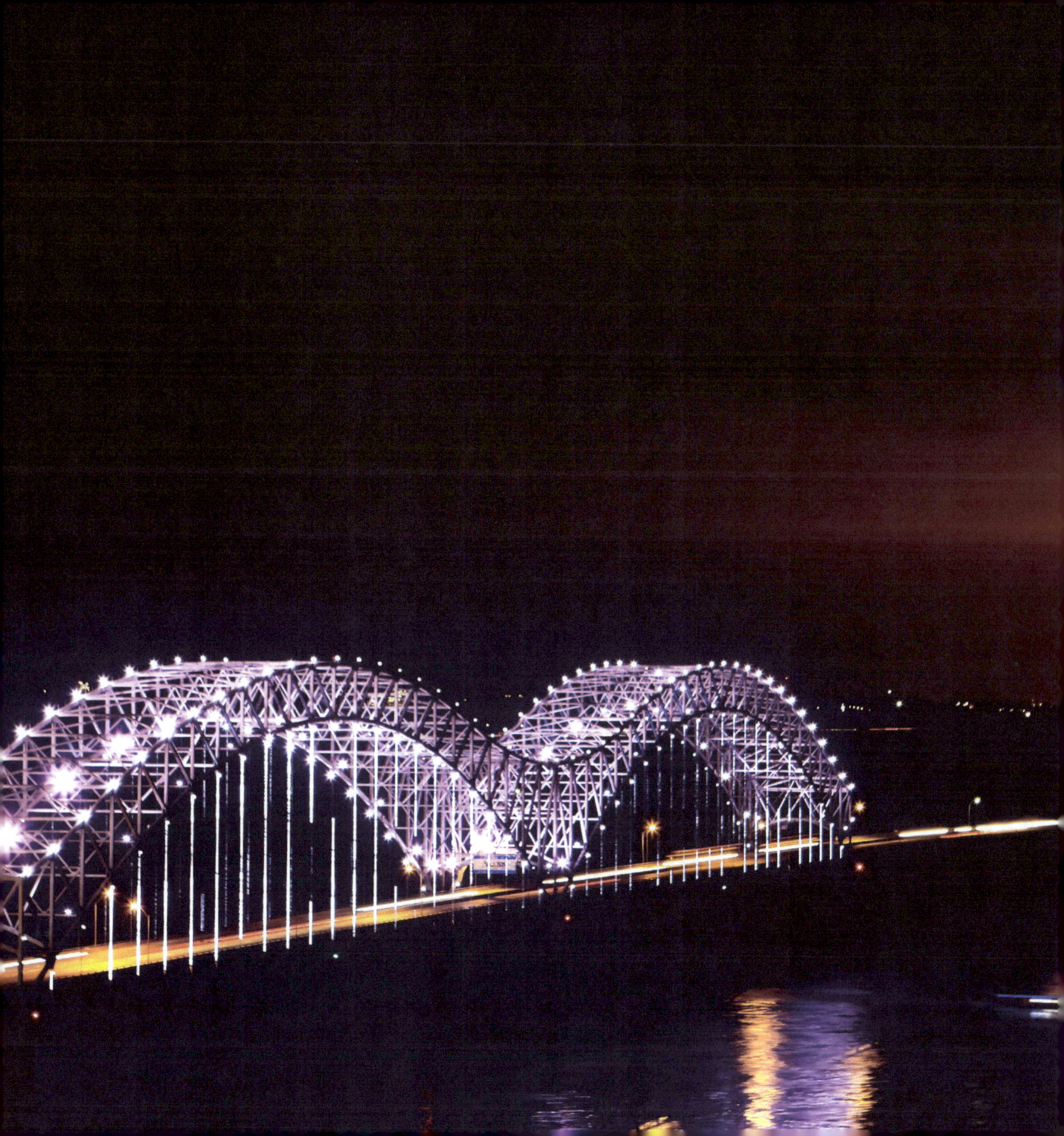

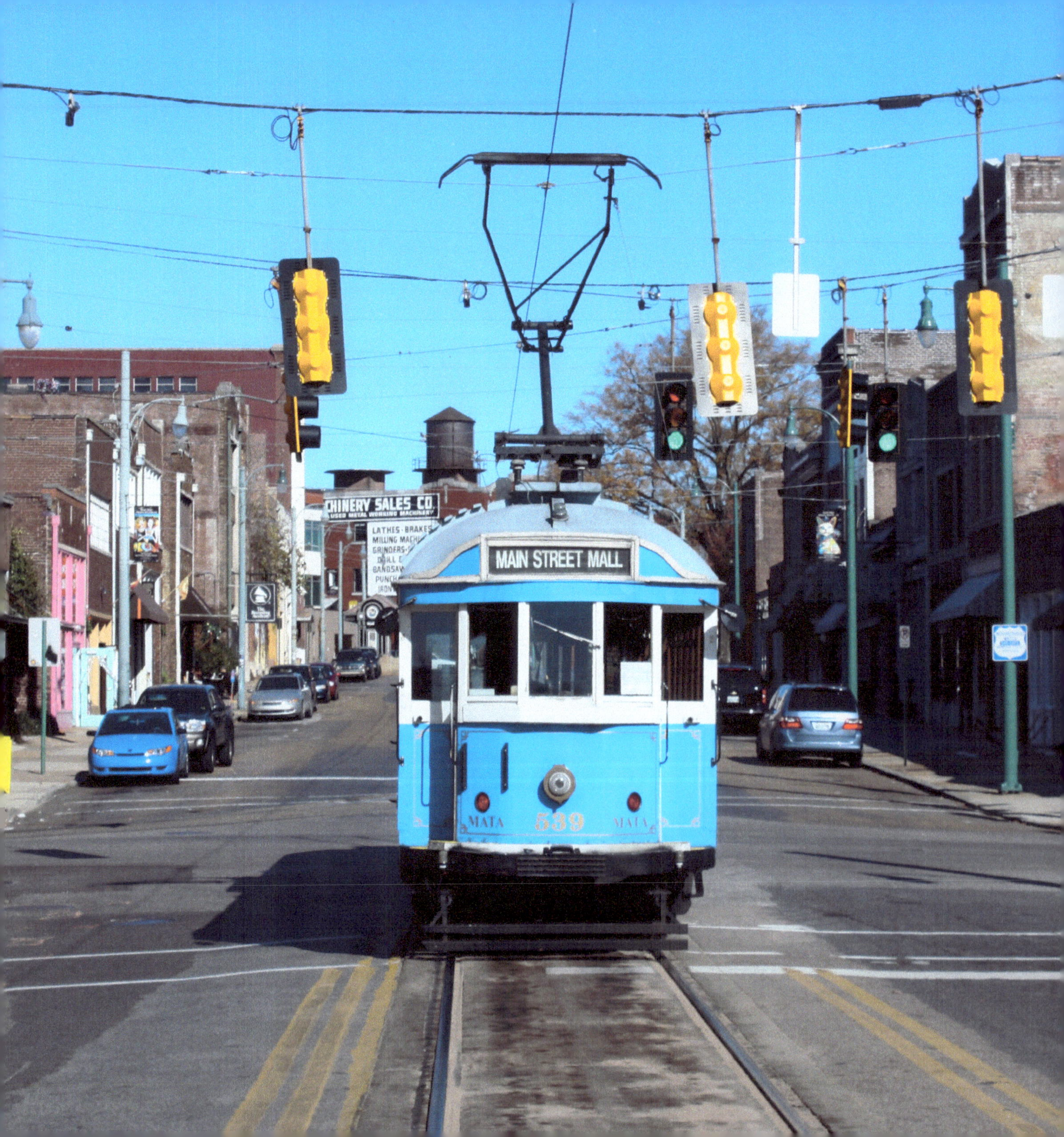
MAIN STREET MALL
MATA 539 MATA
LATHES-BRAKES

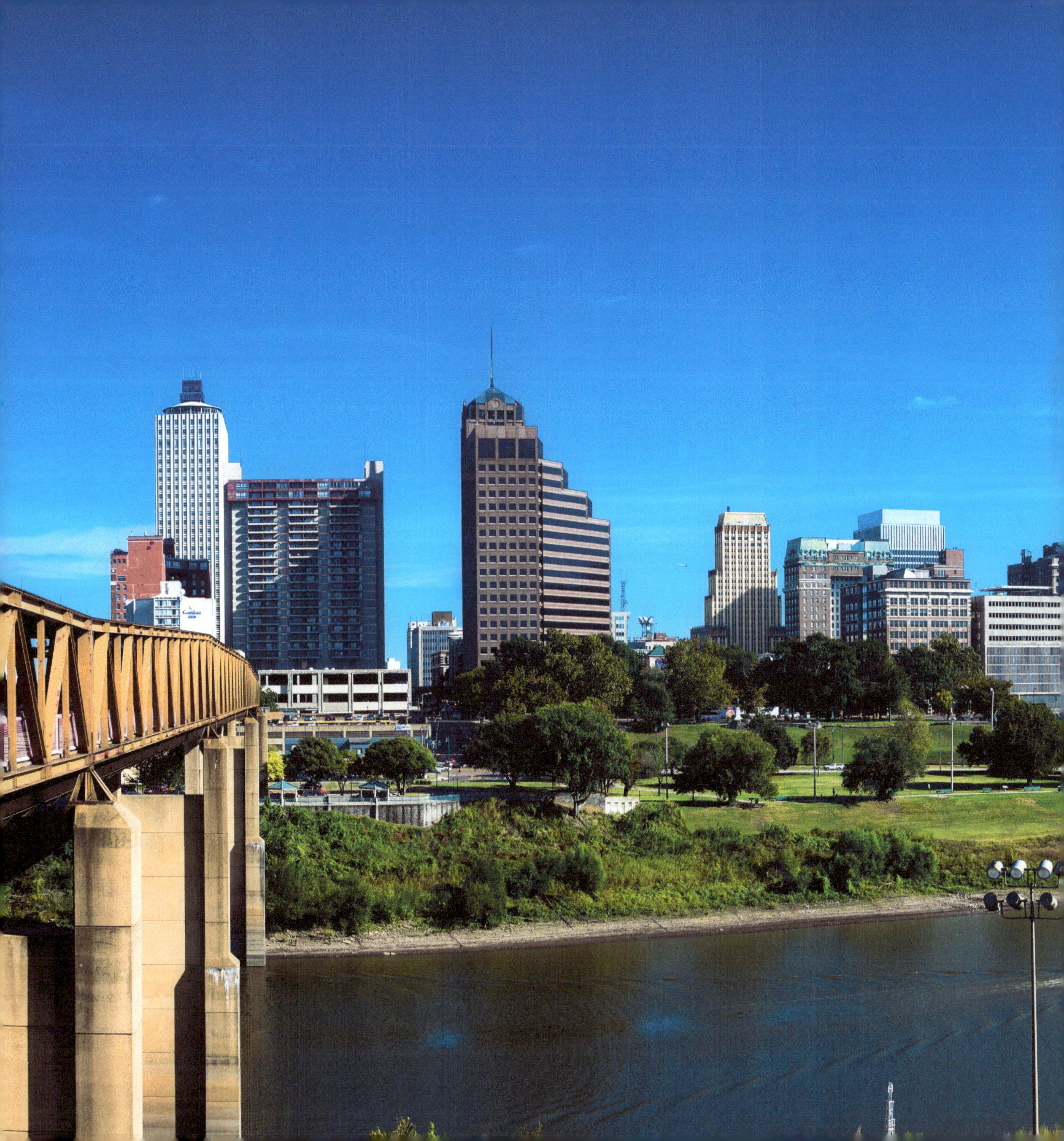

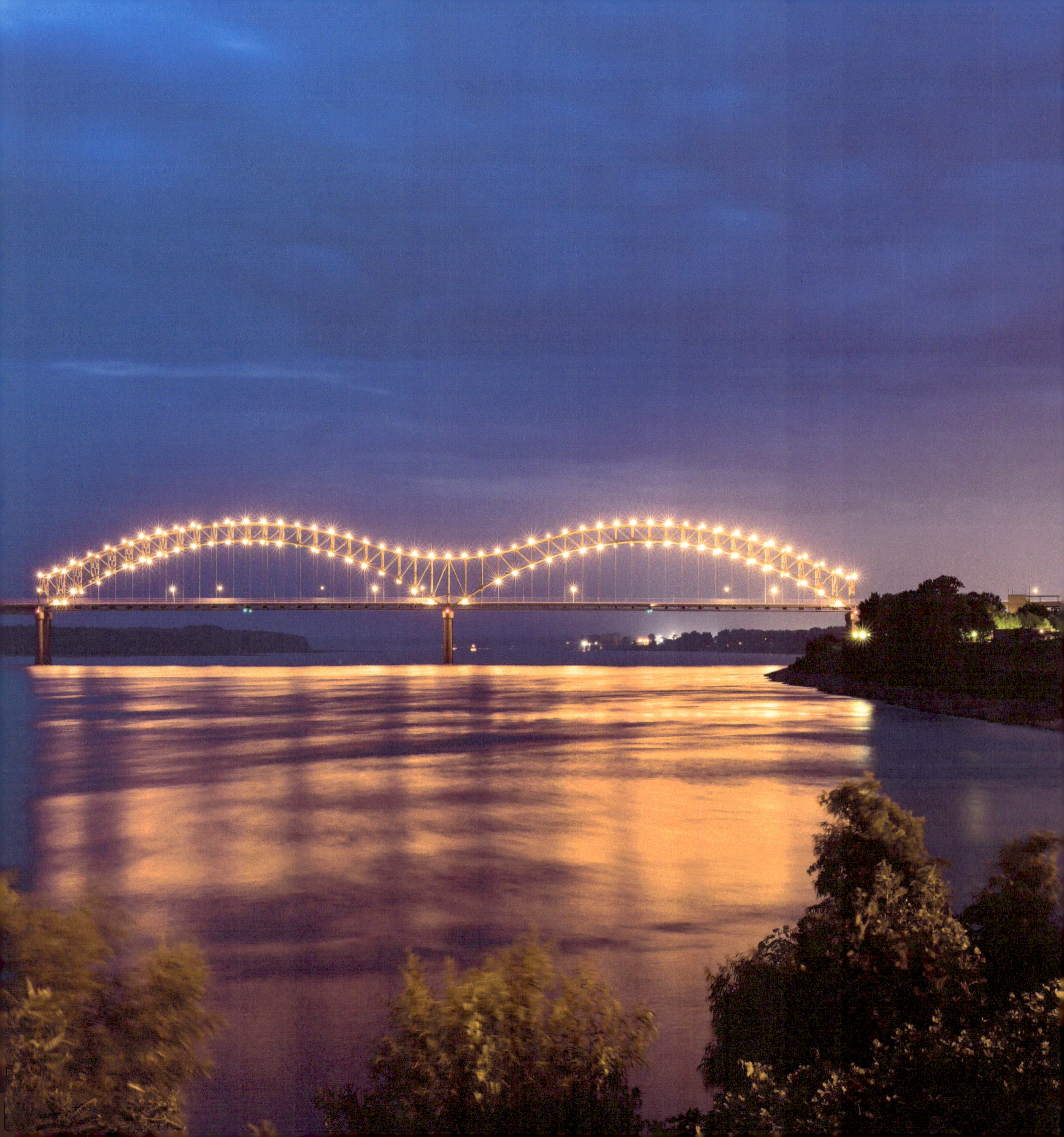

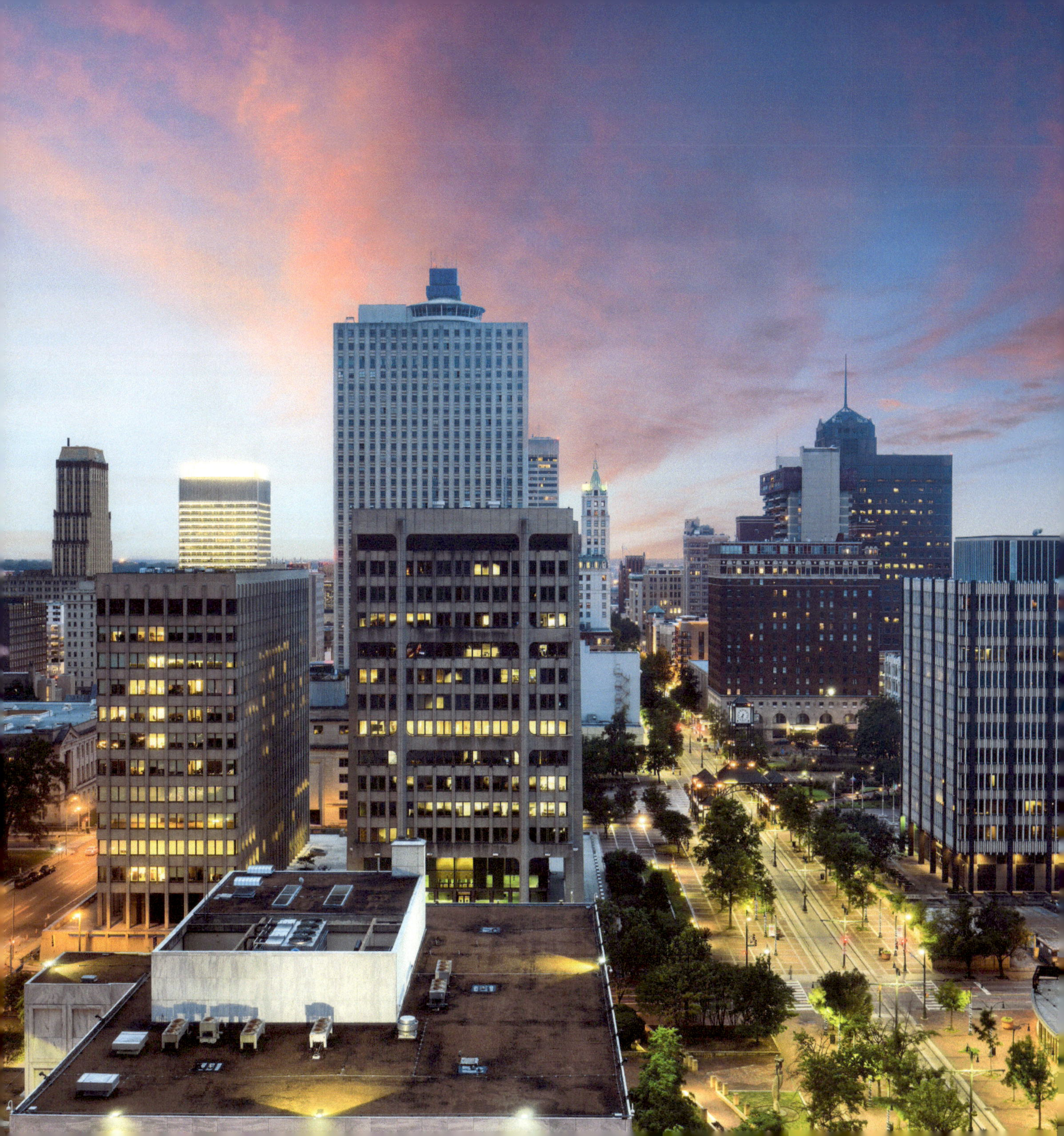

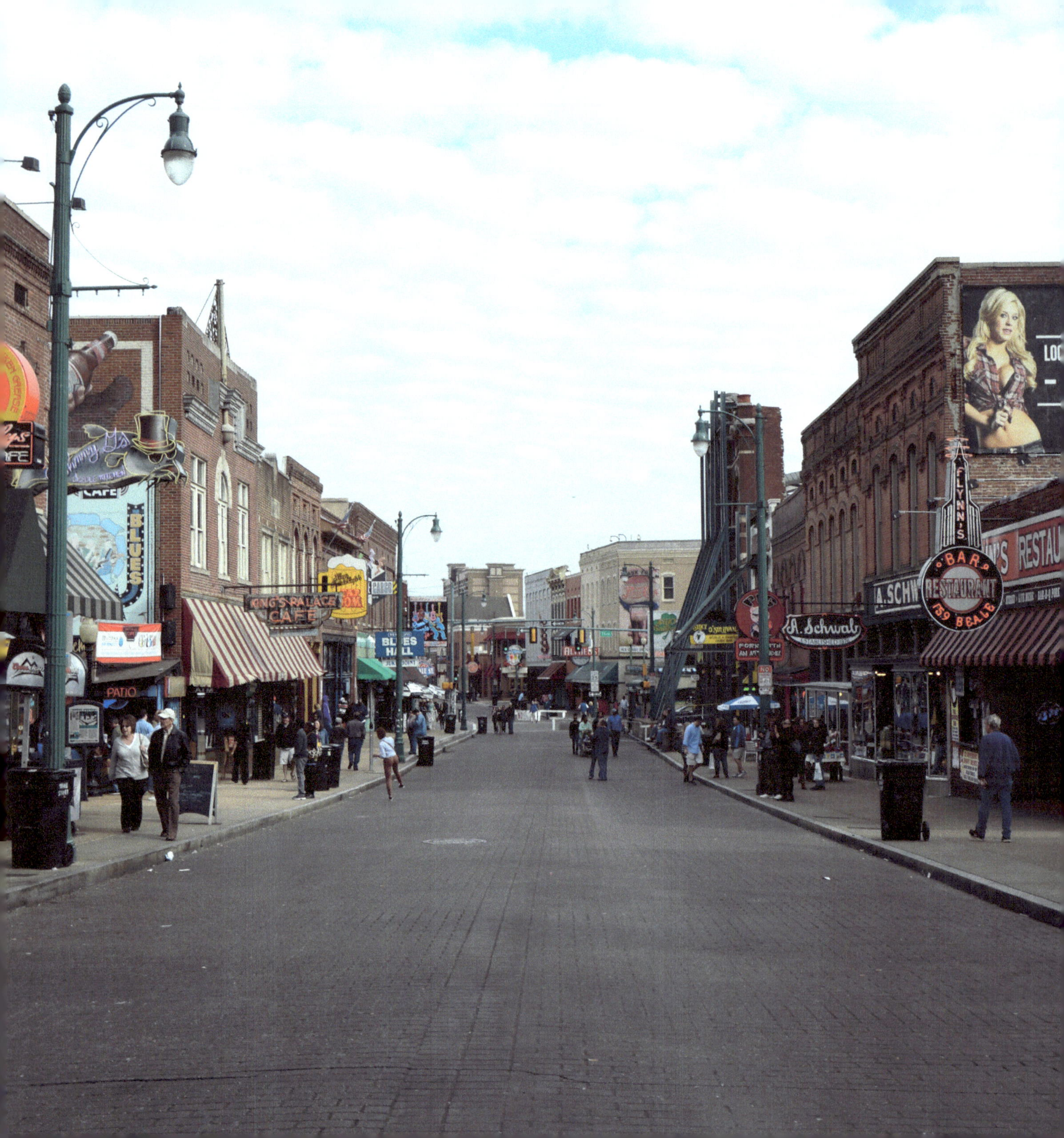
KING'S PALACE
CAFE
BLUES
BLUES HALL
PATIO
FLYNN'S
BAR
RESTAURANT
139 BEALE
A. Schwab
A. SCHW

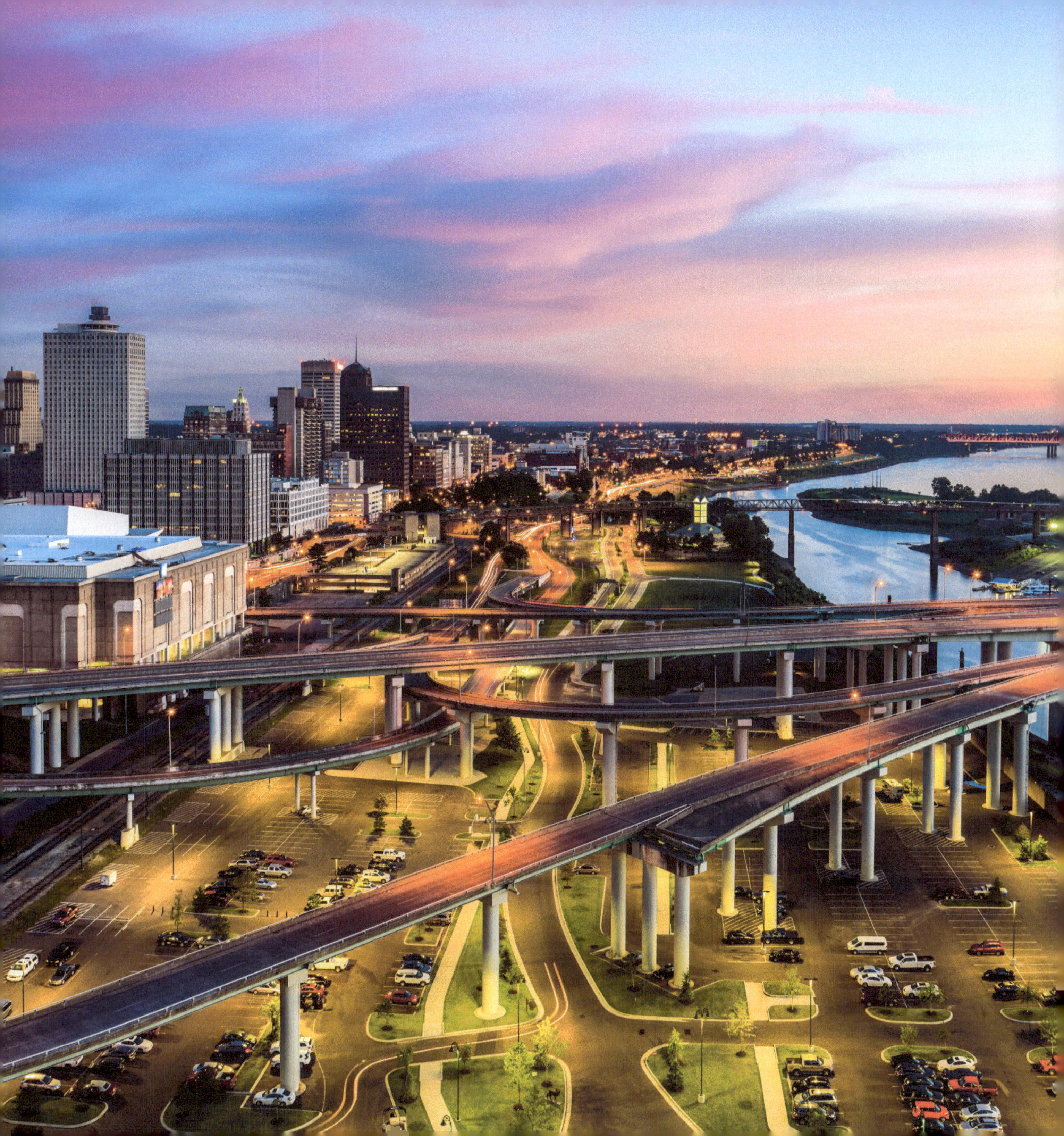

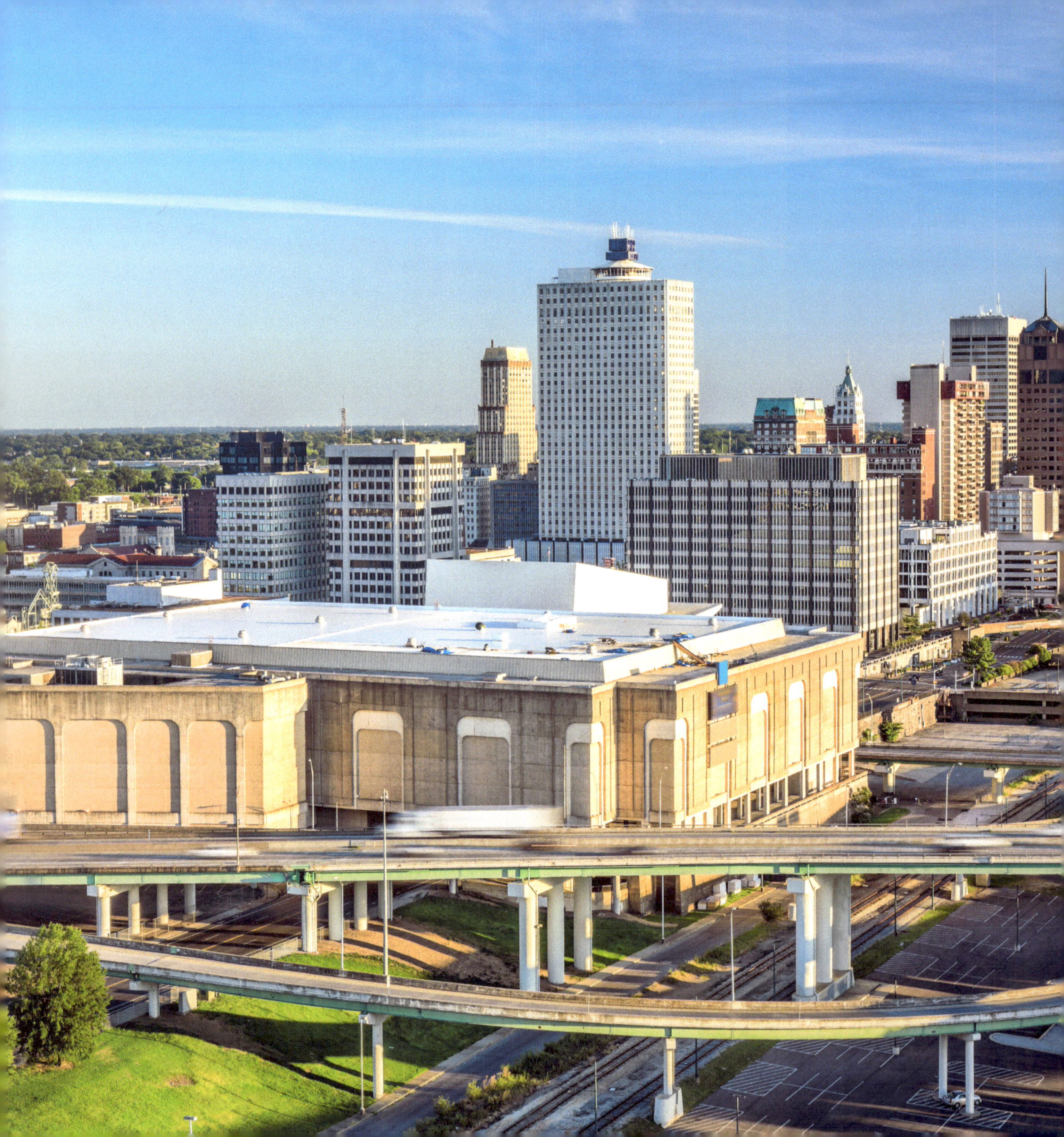

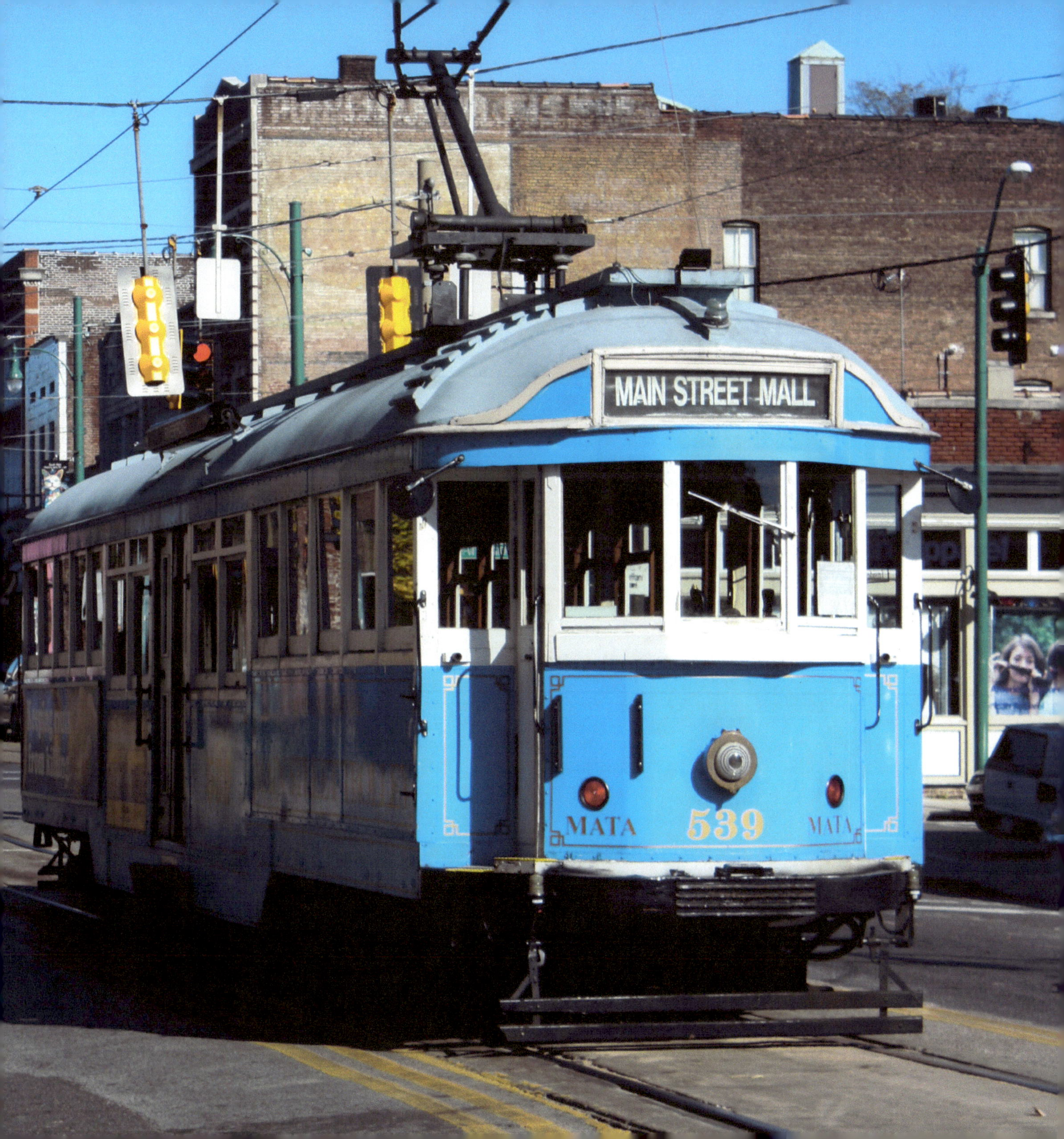
MAIN STREET MALL
MATA
539
MATA

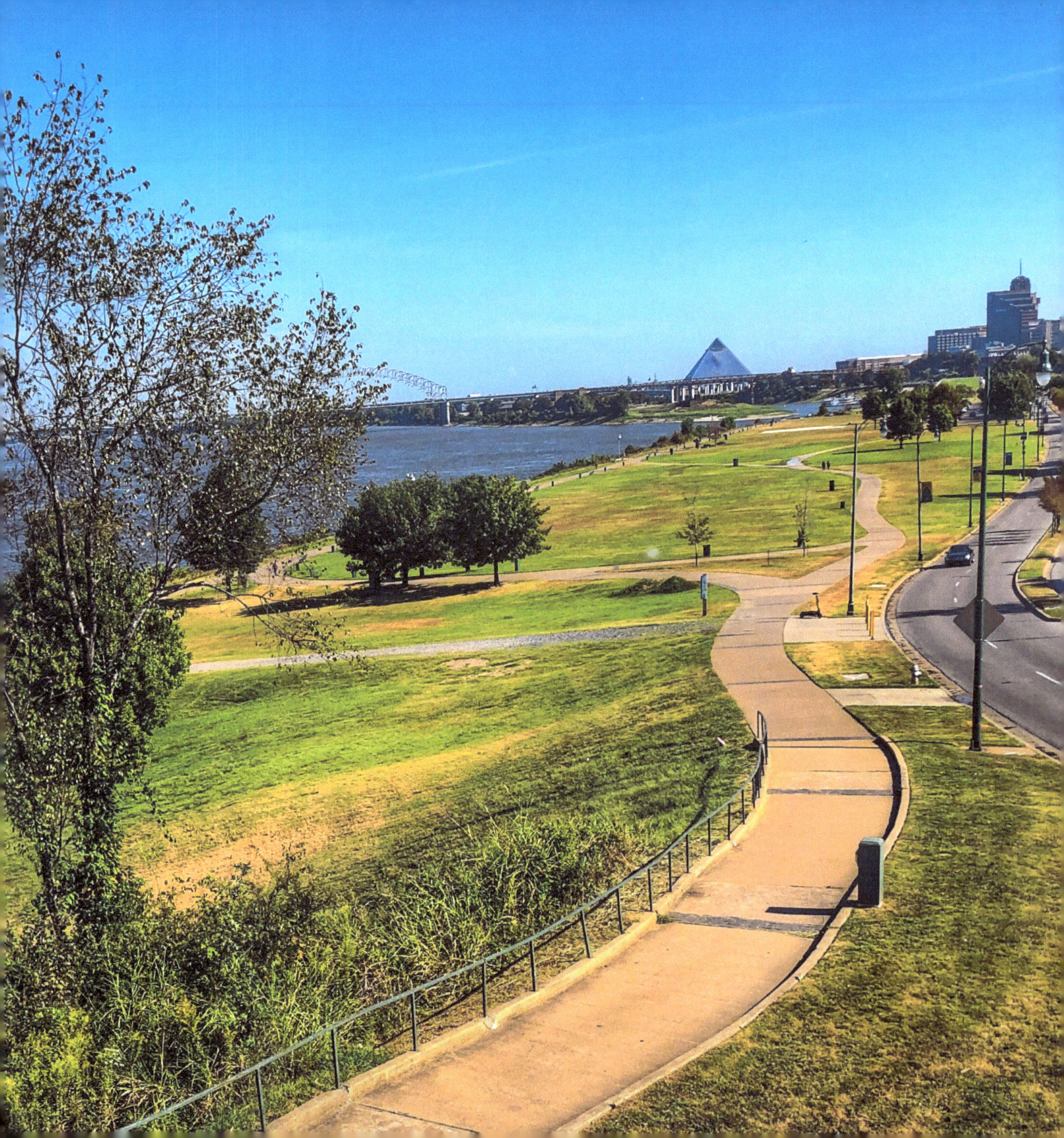

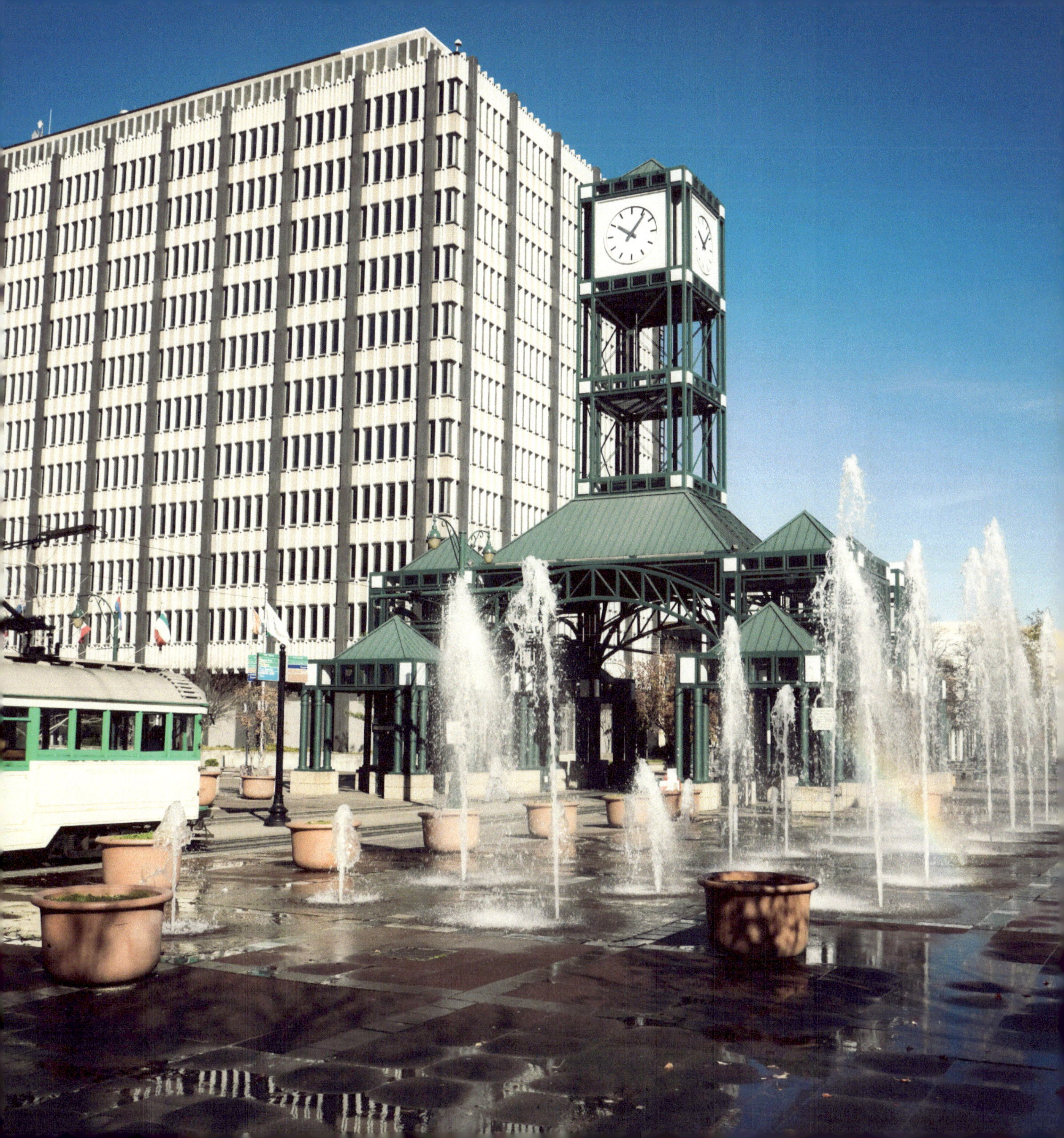

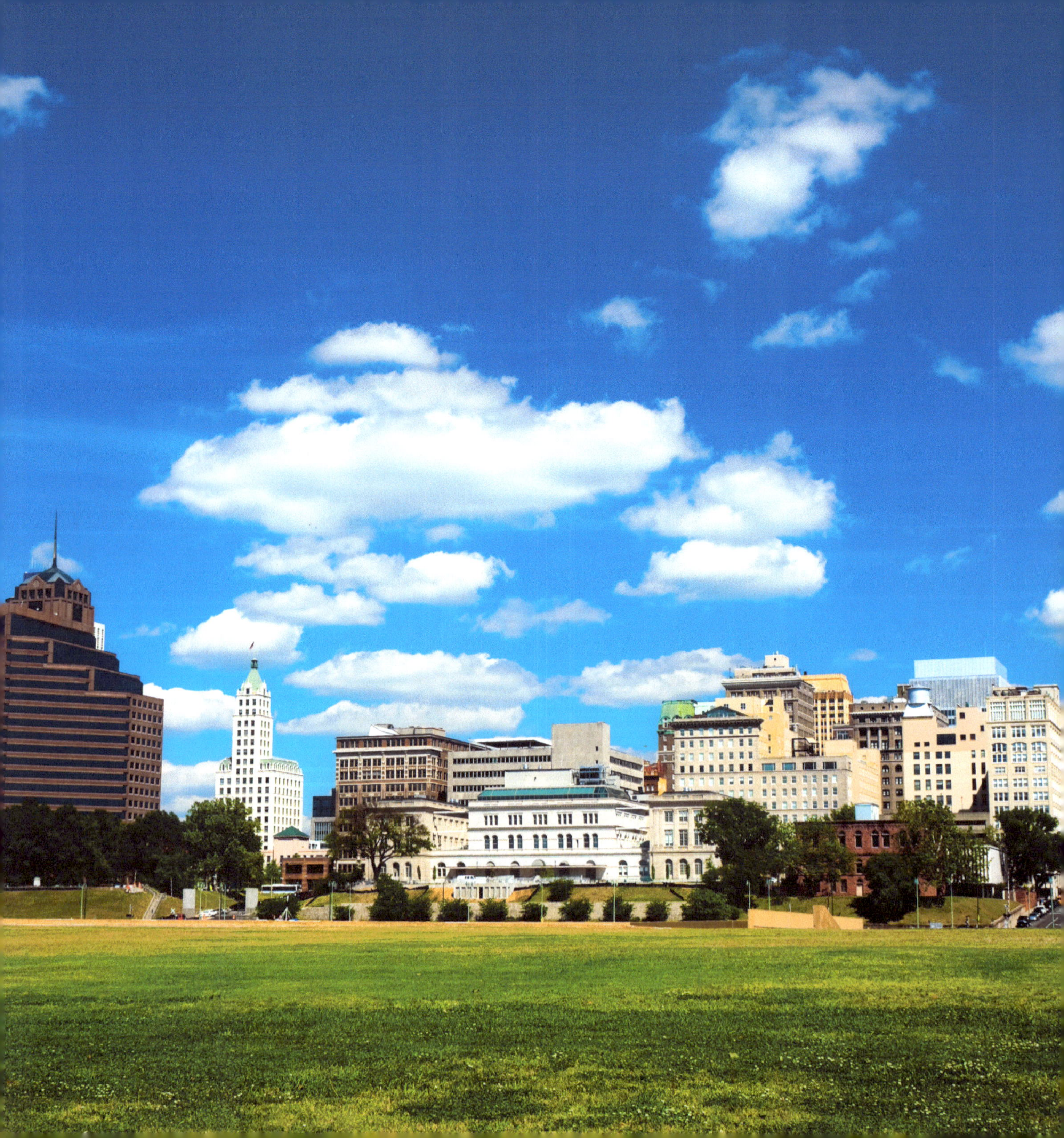

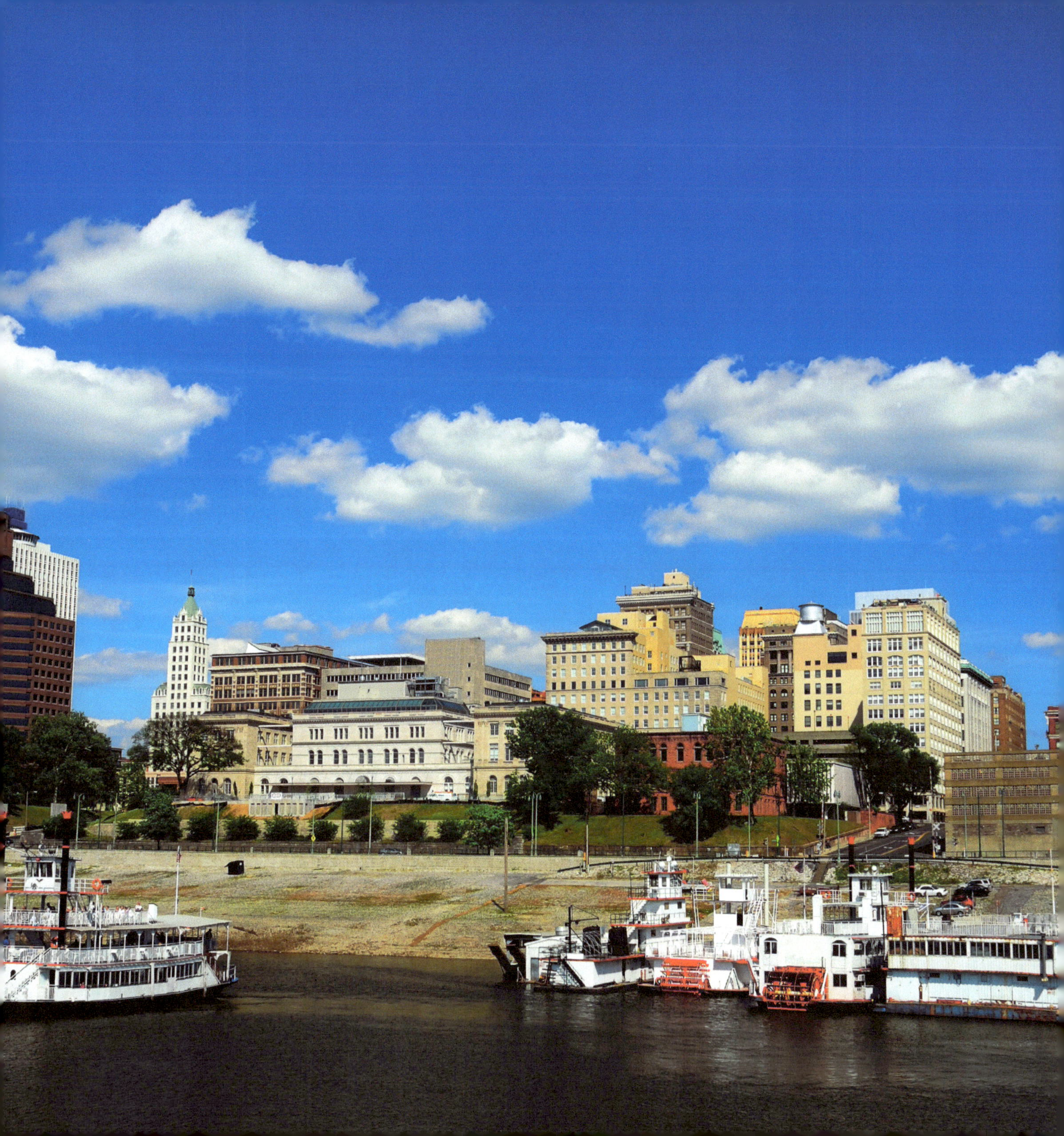

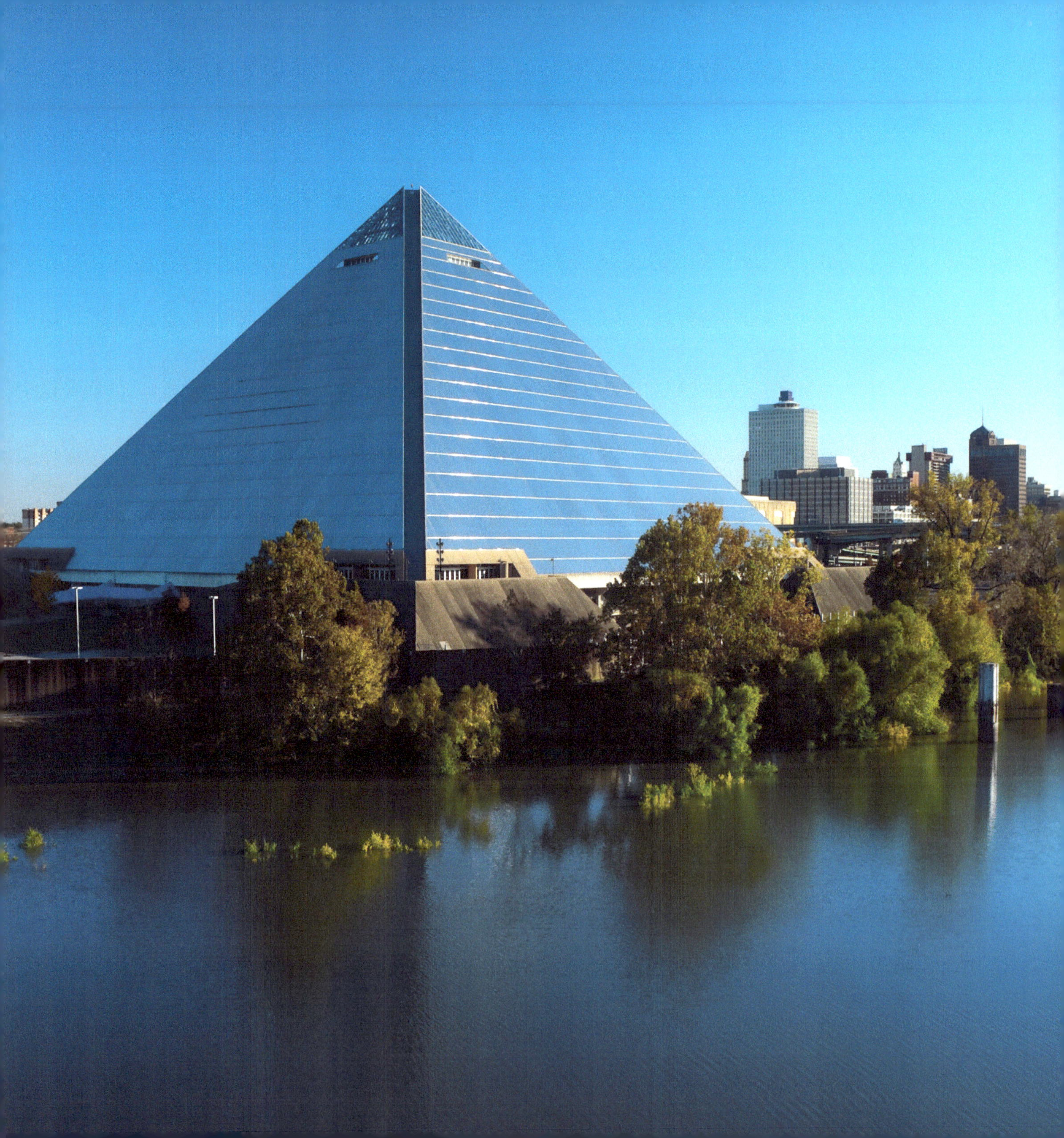

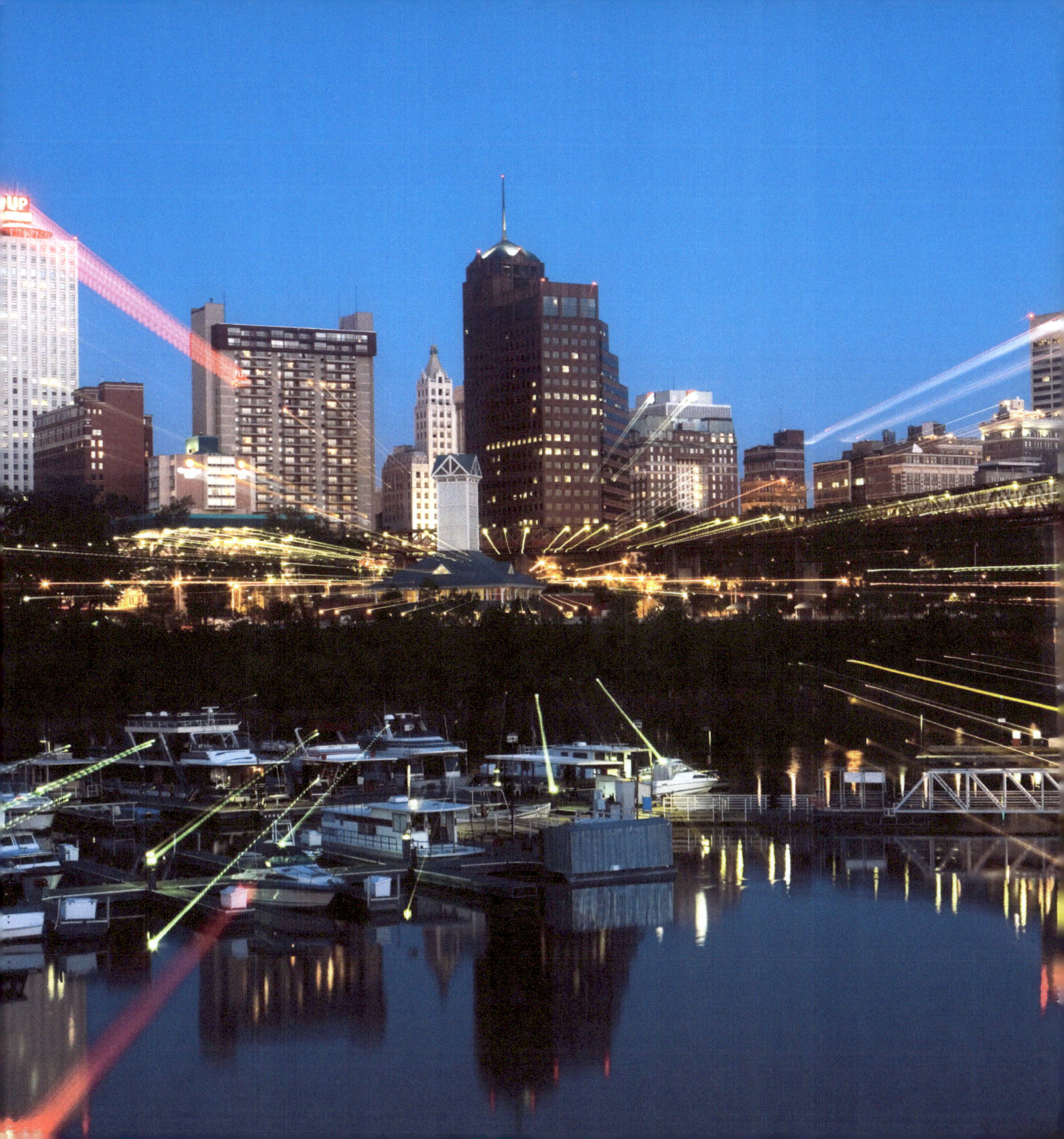

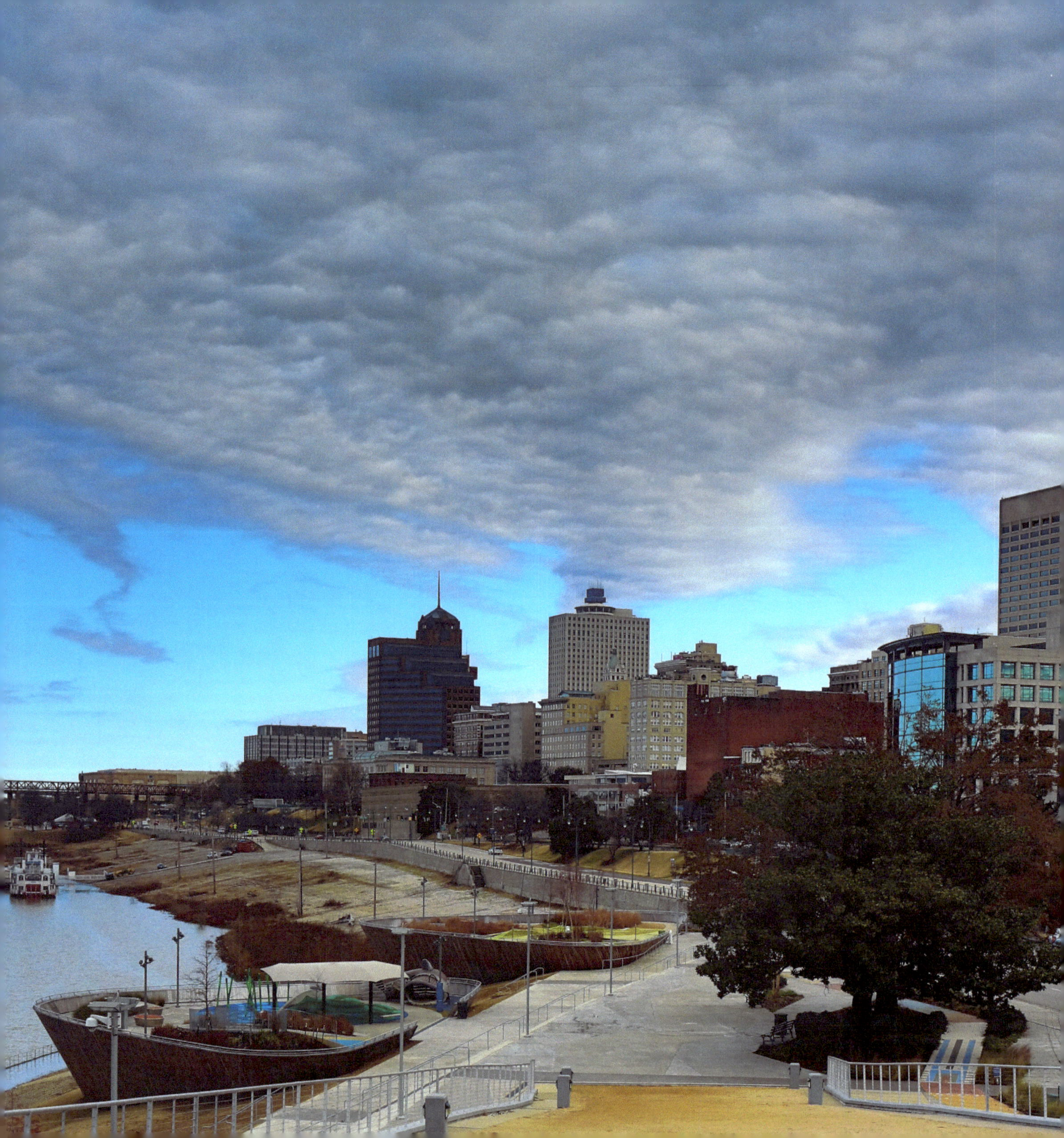

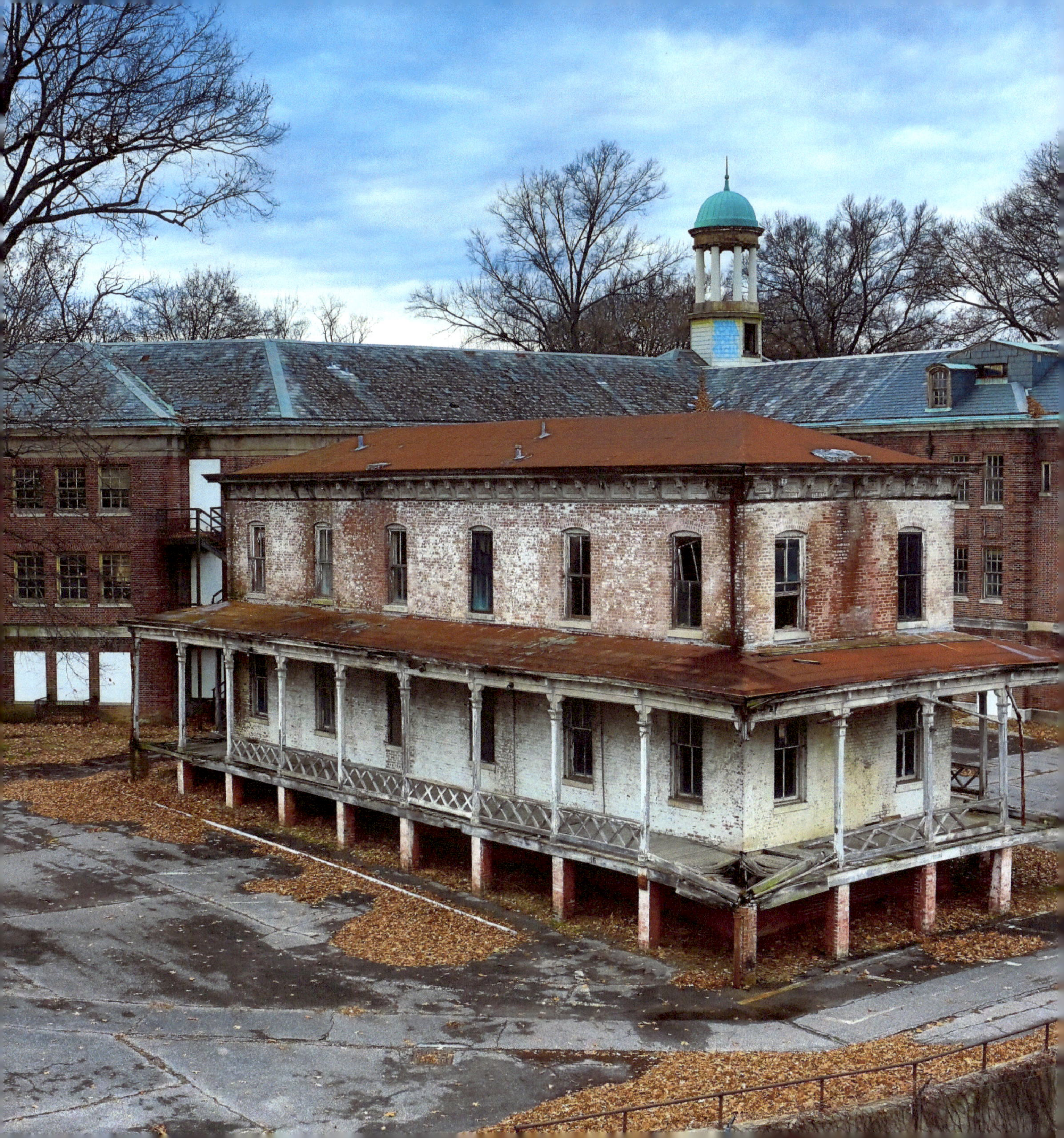

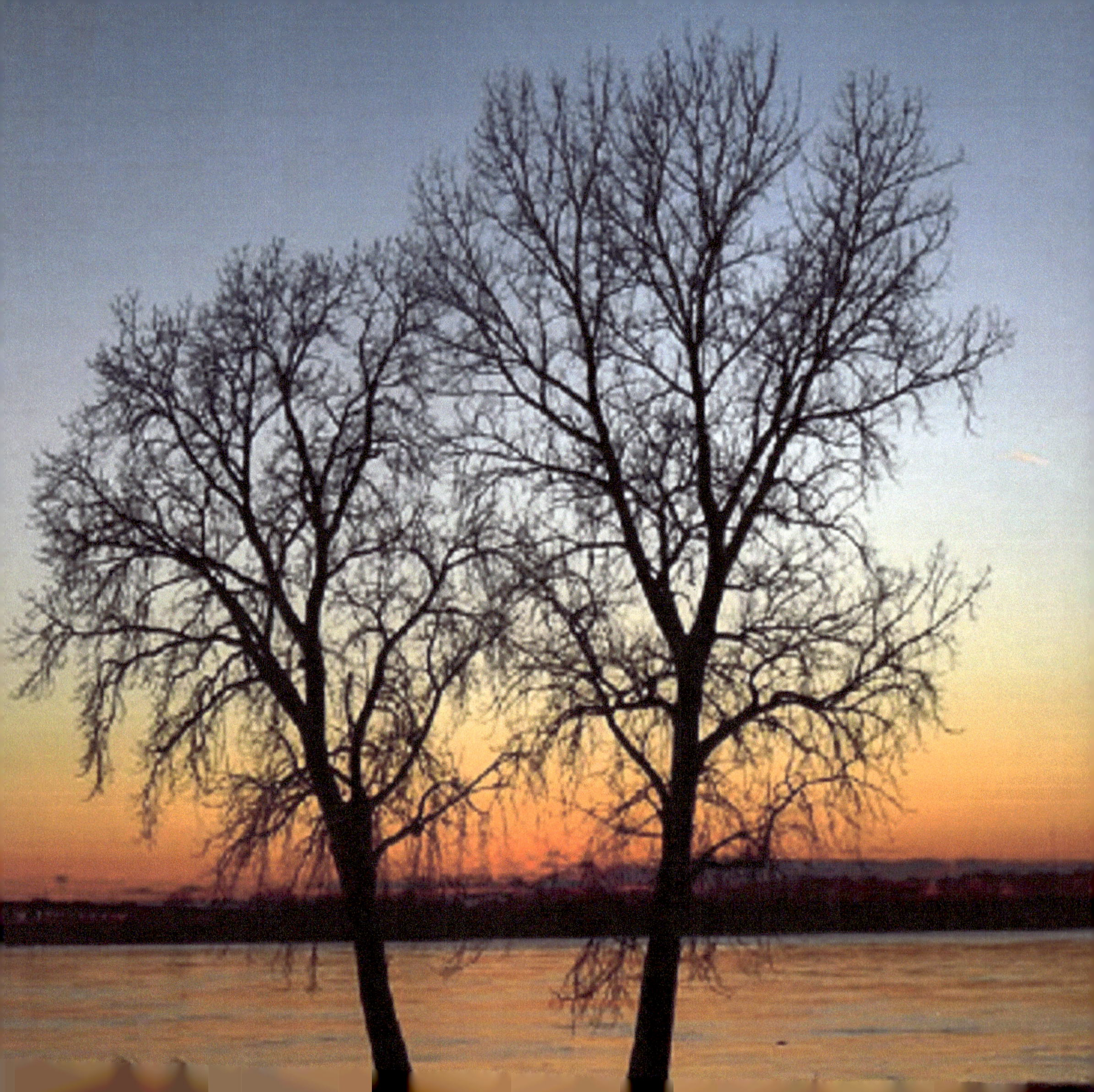

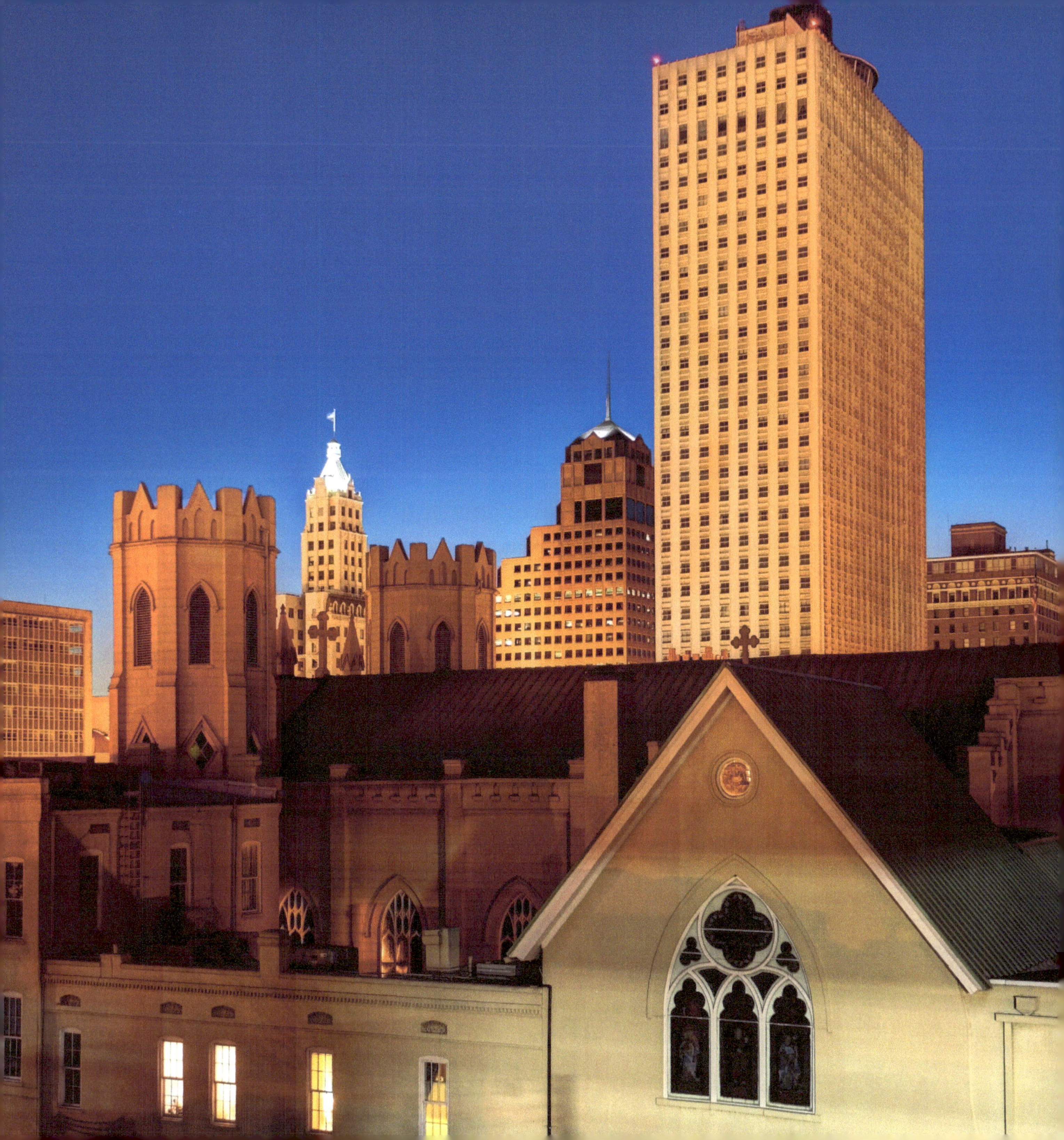

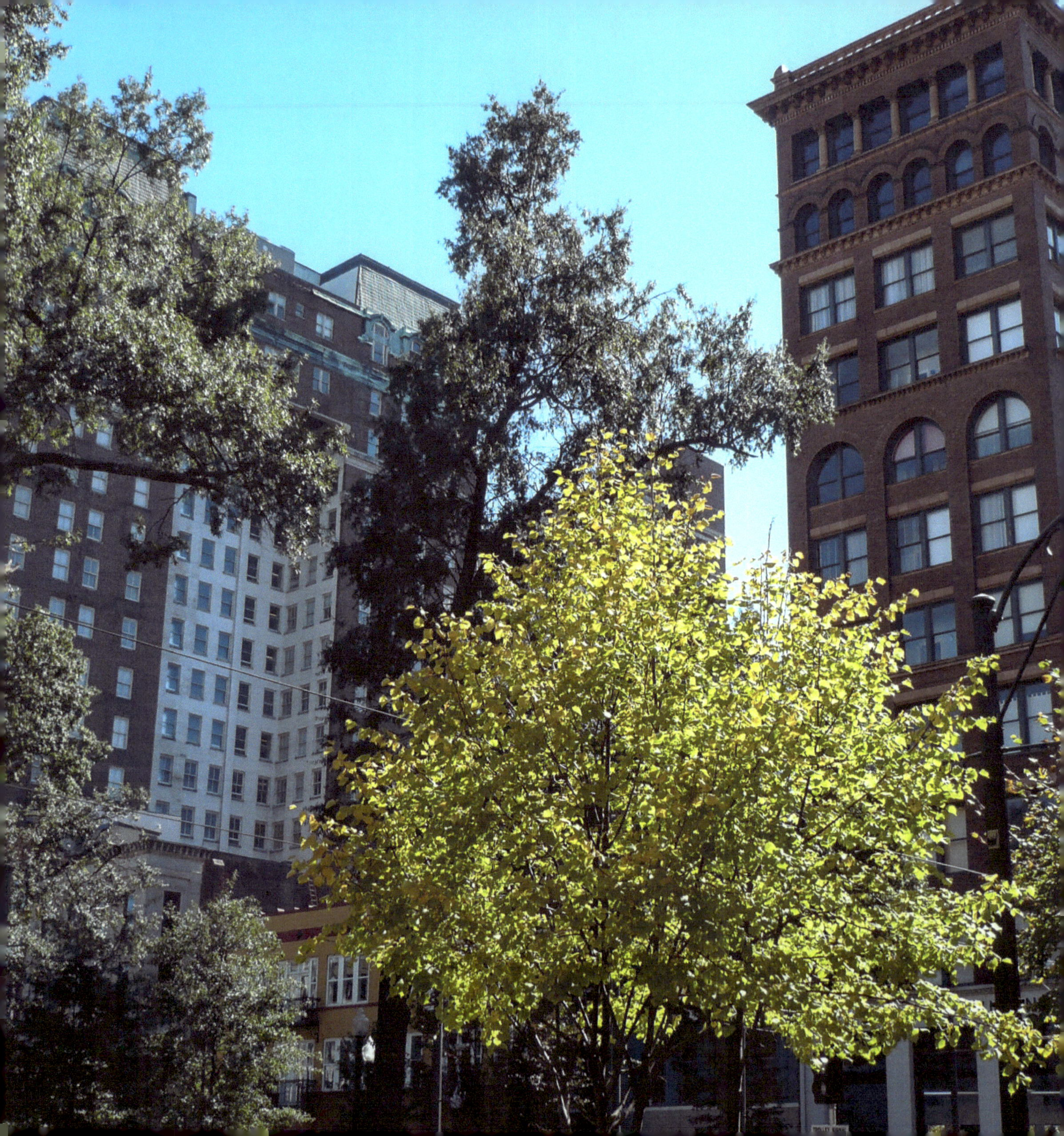

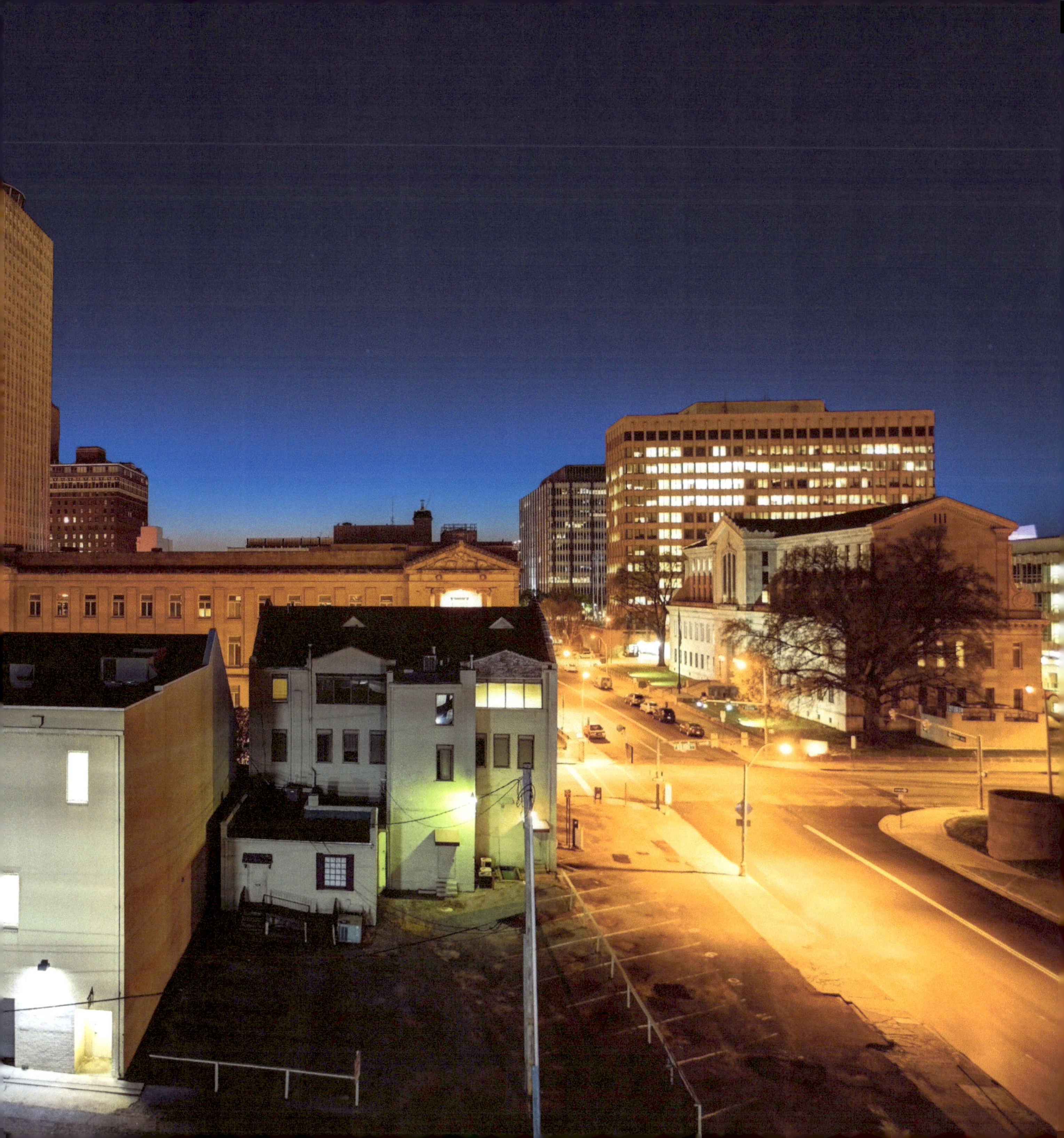

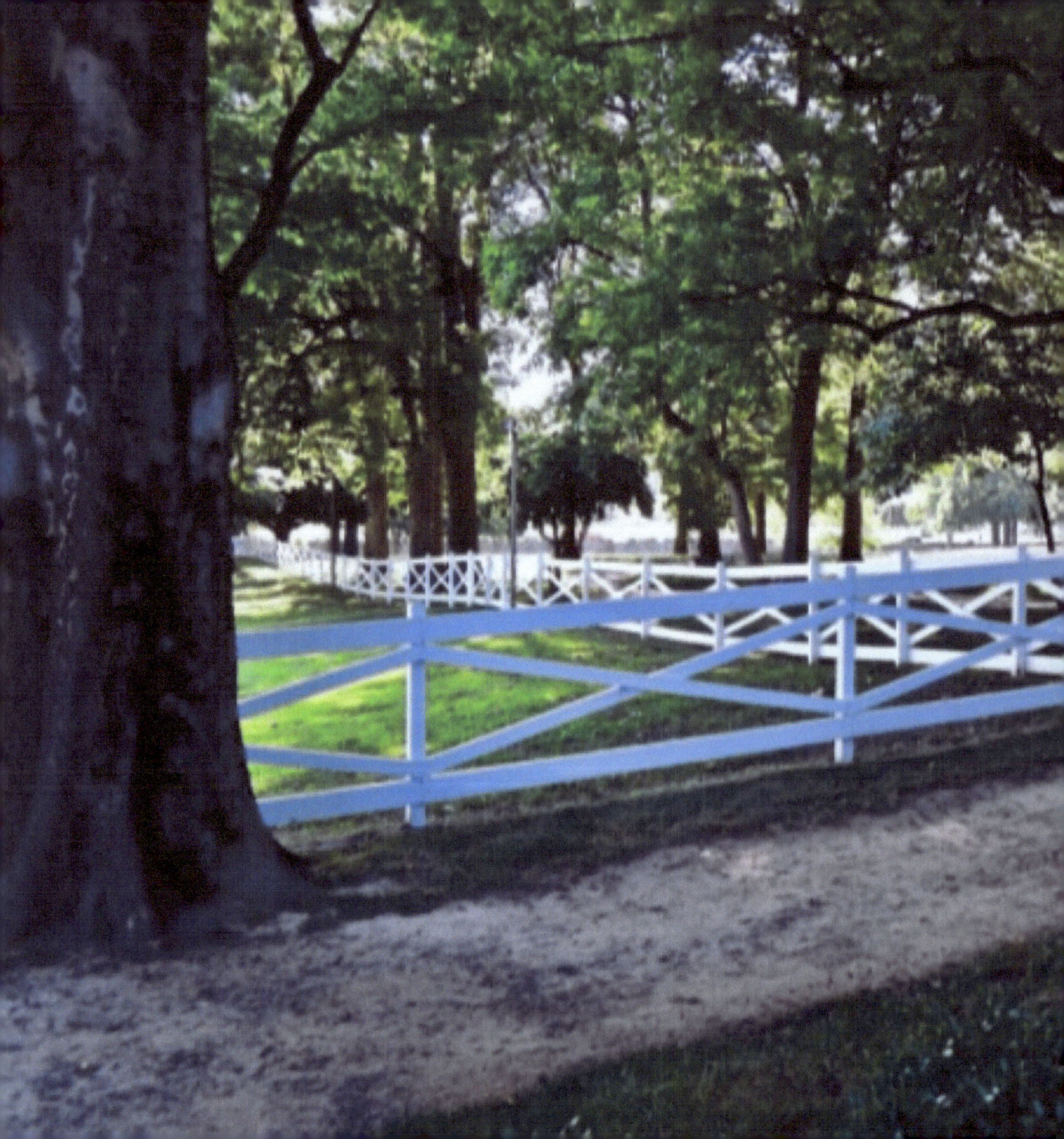

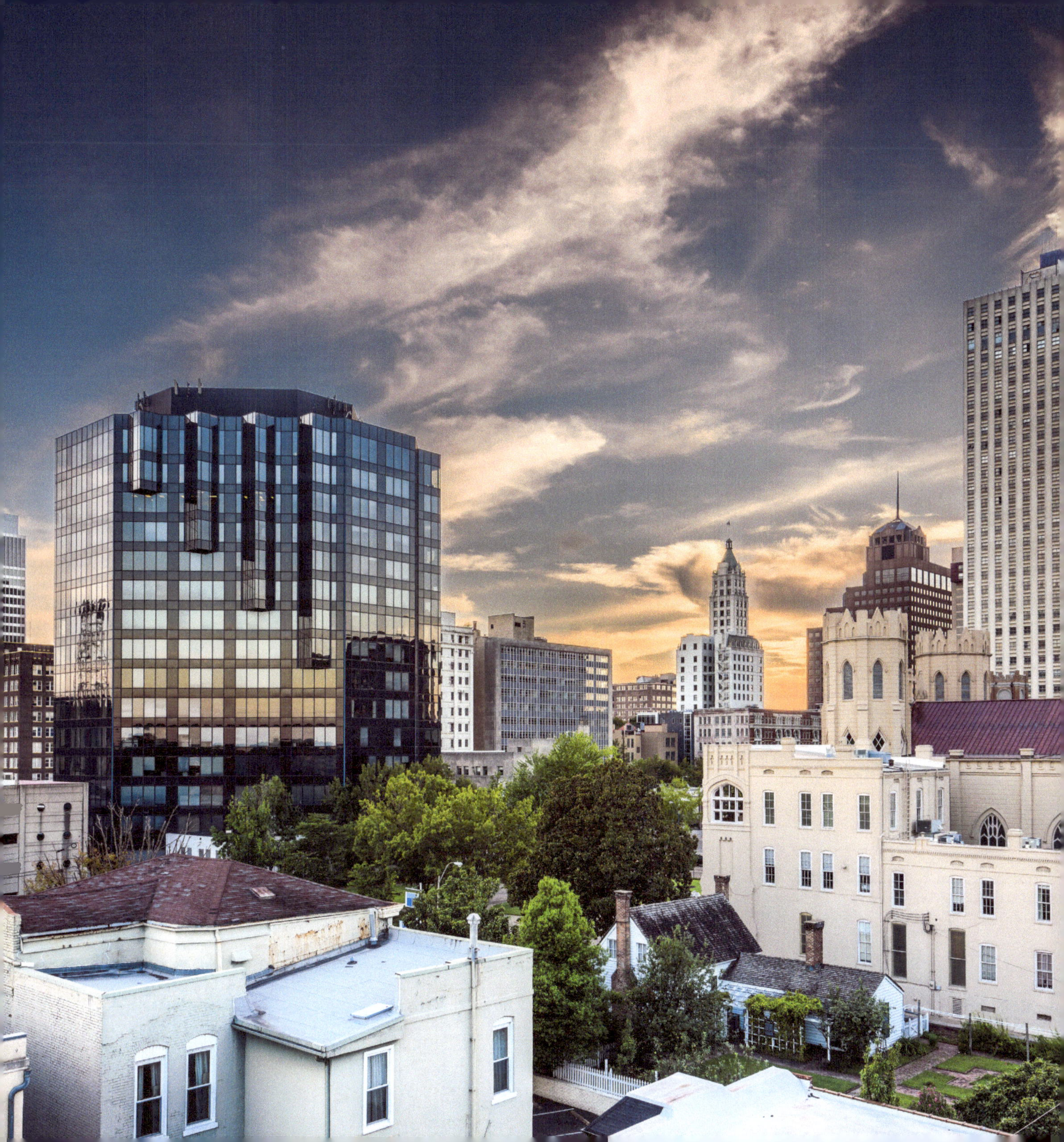

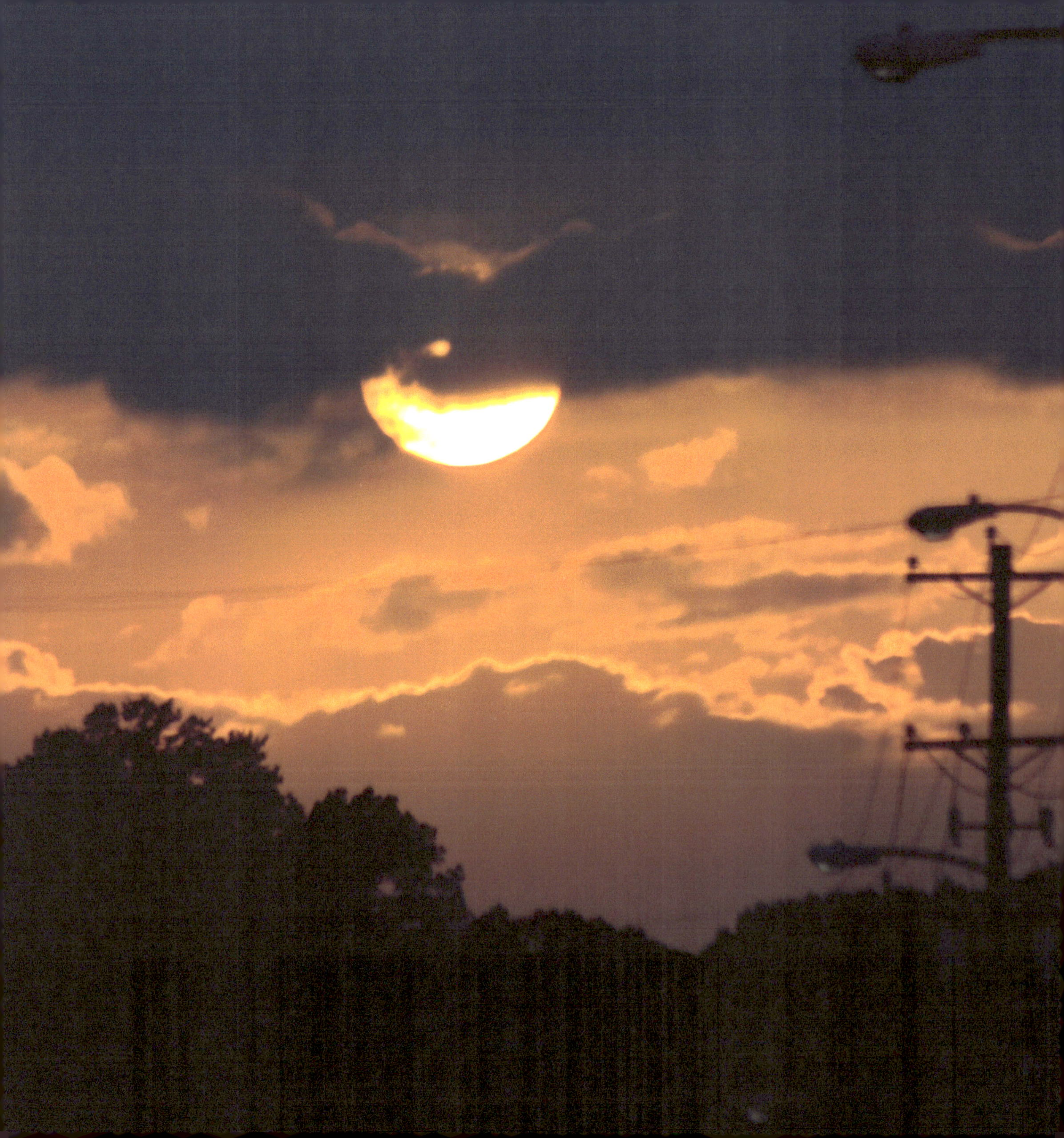

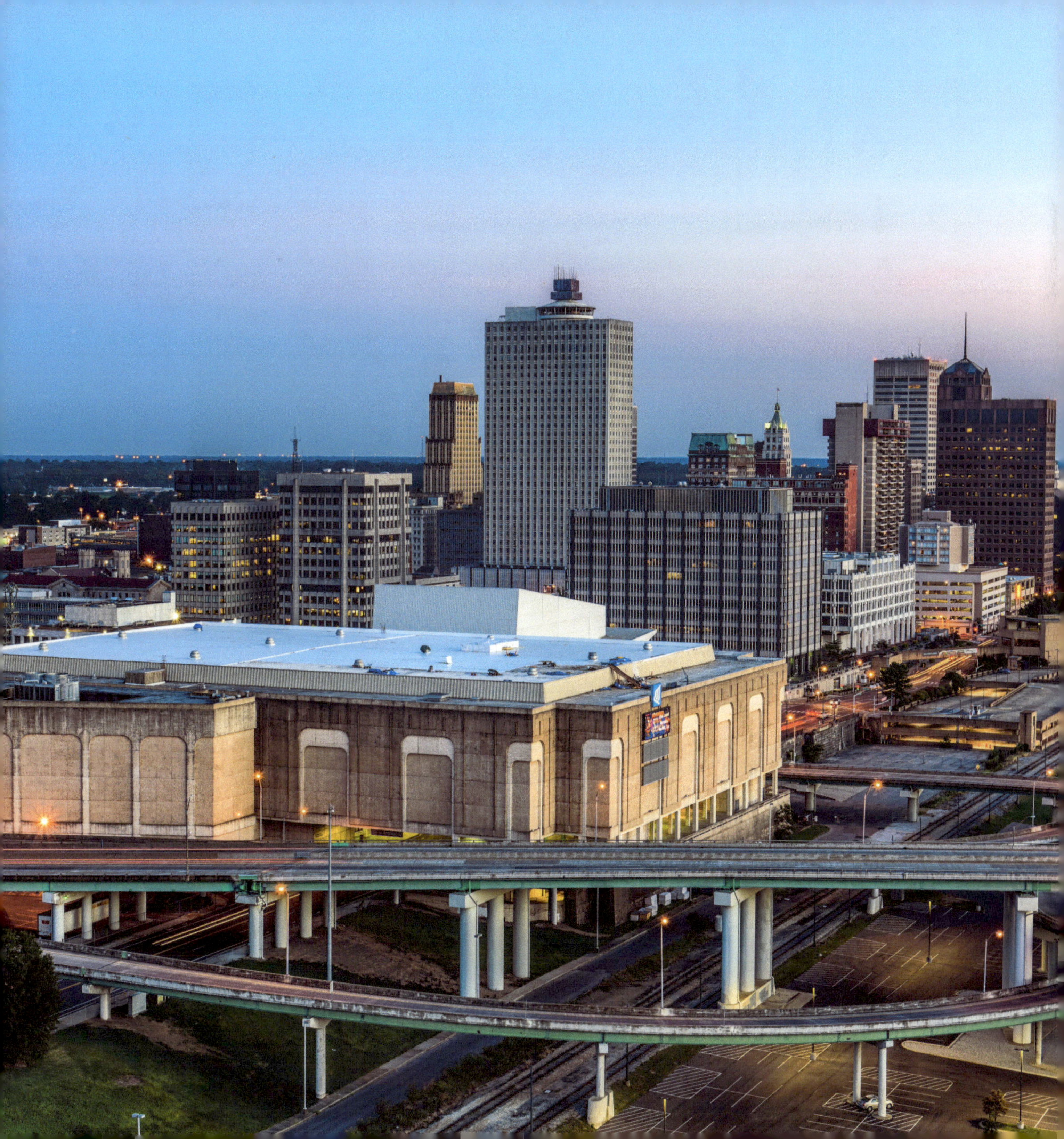

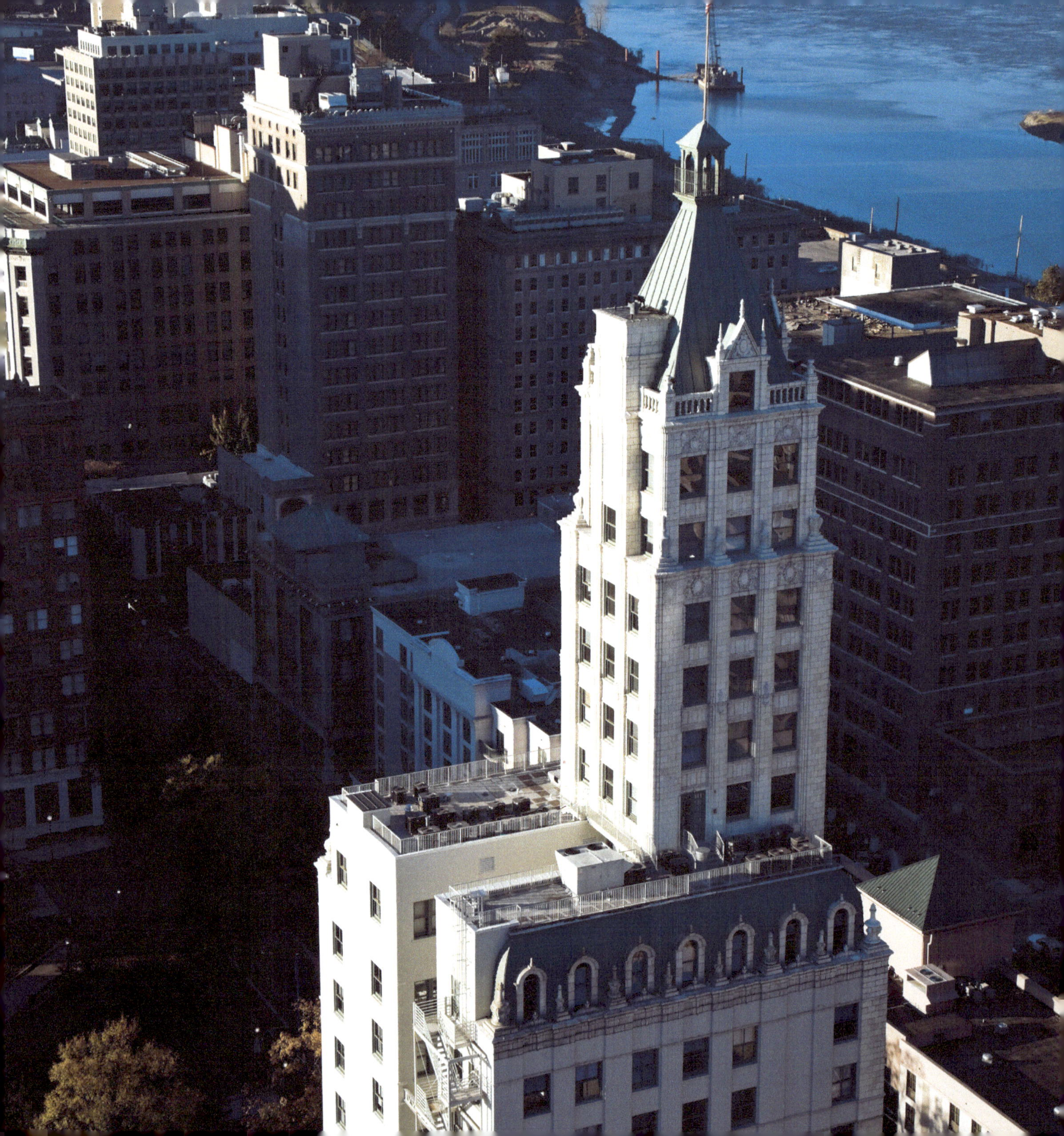

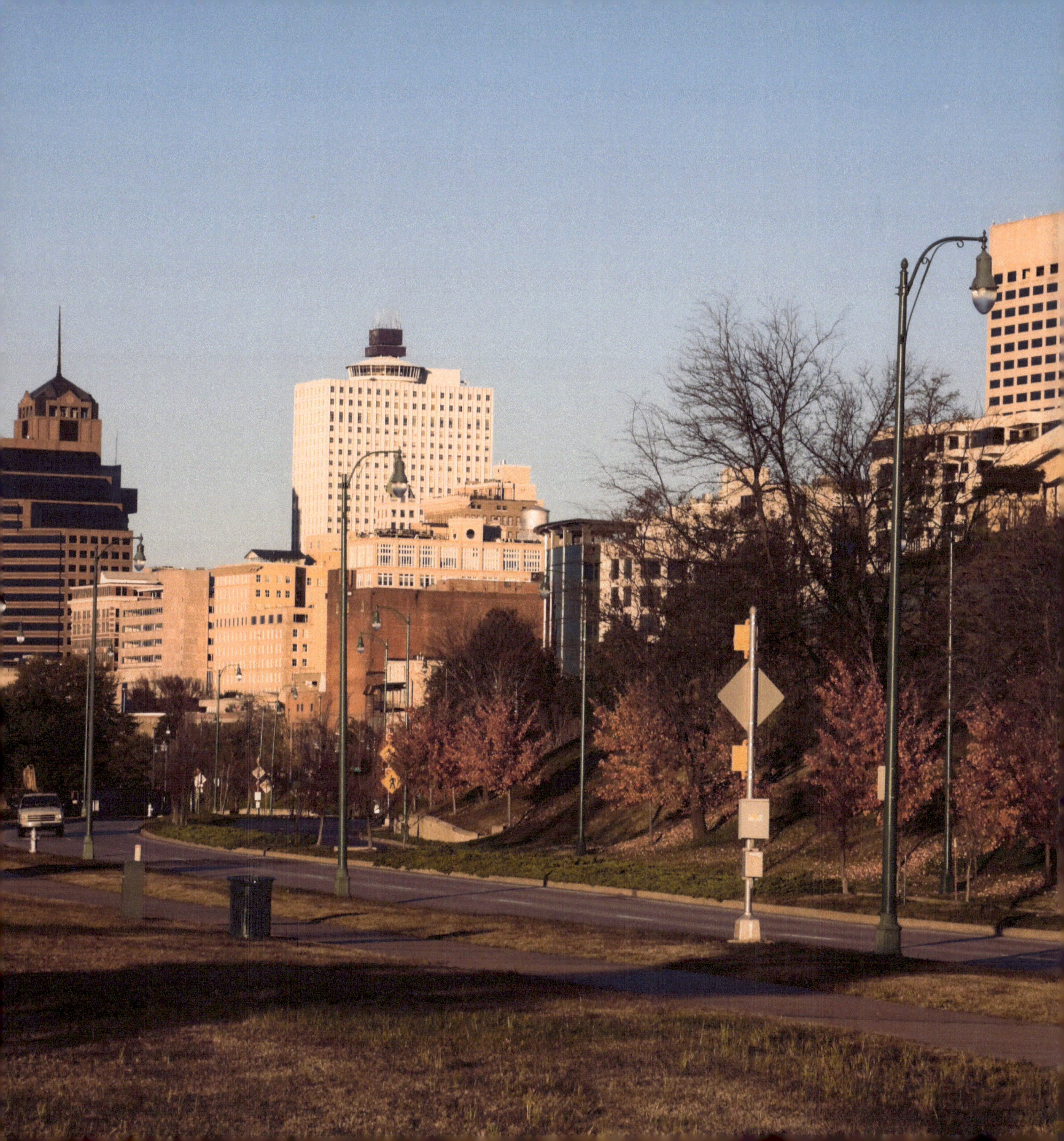

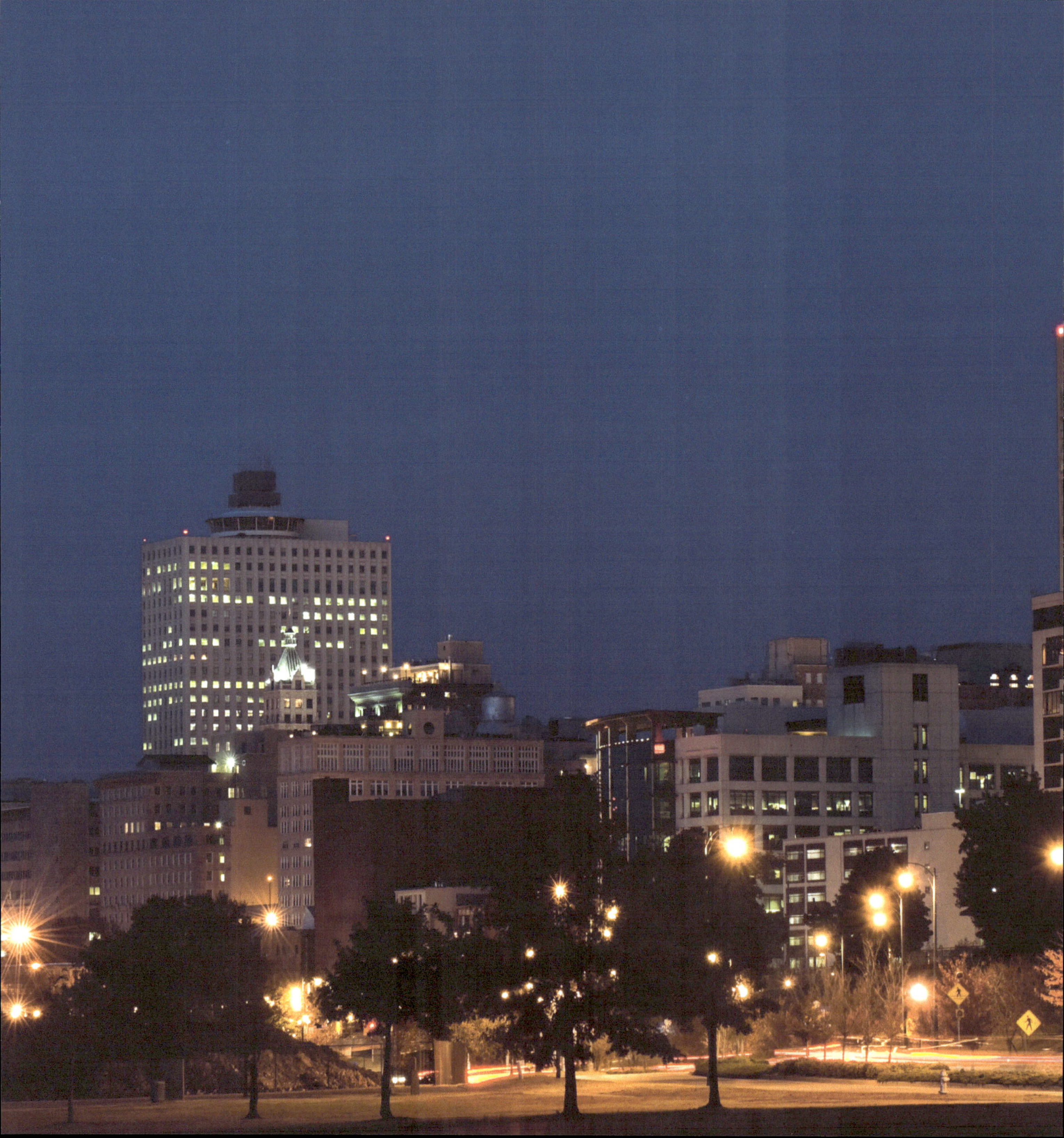

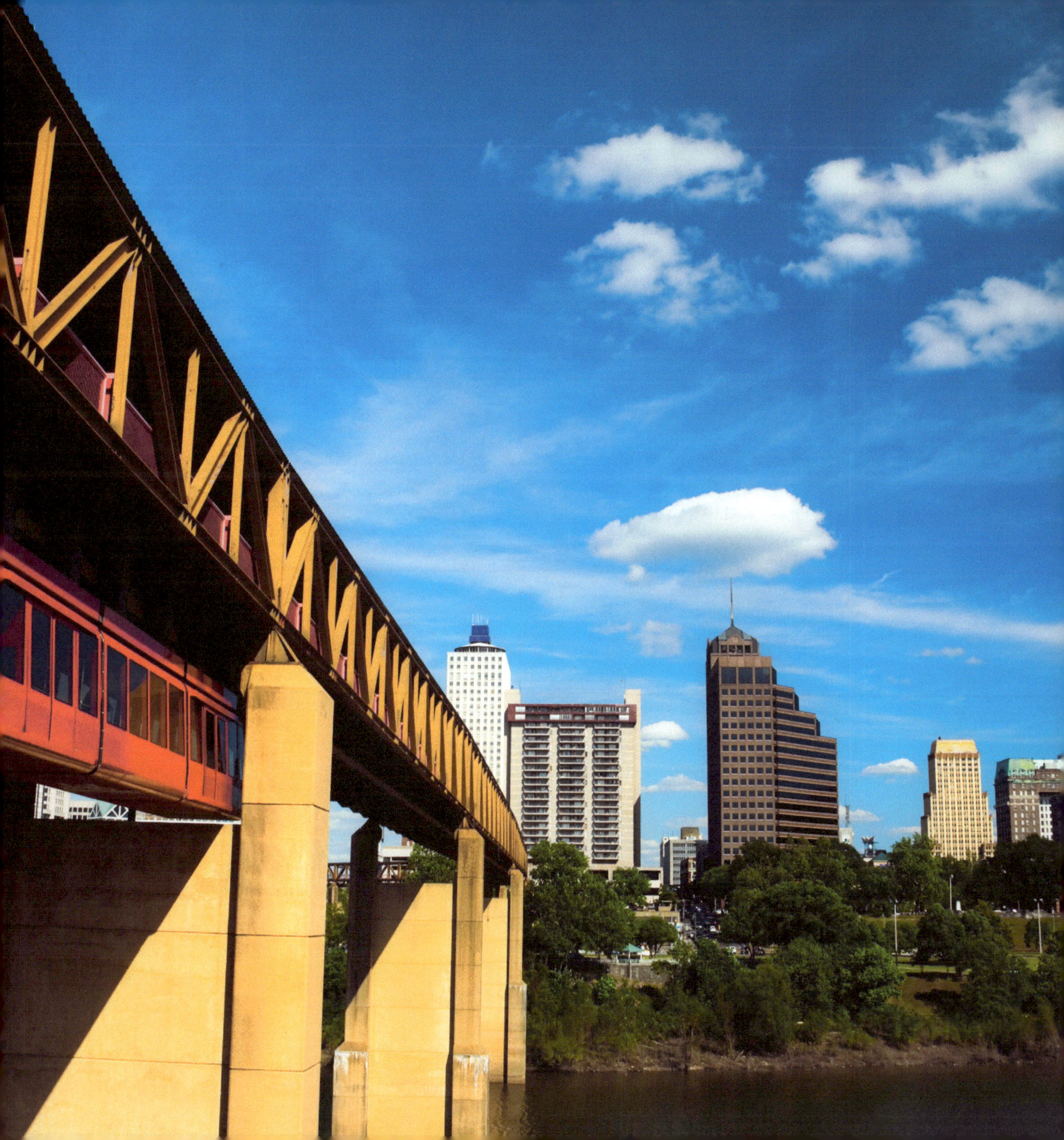

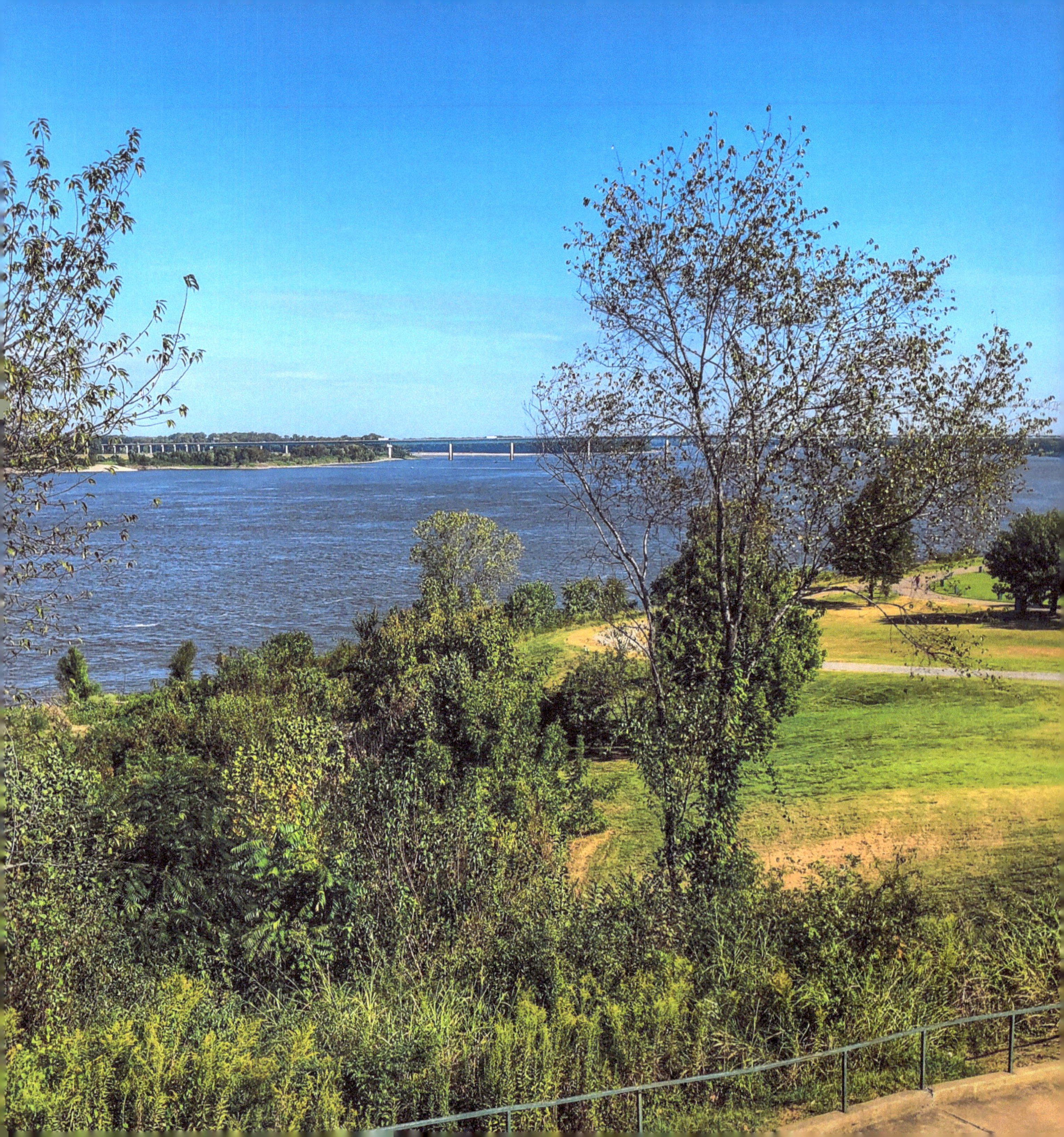

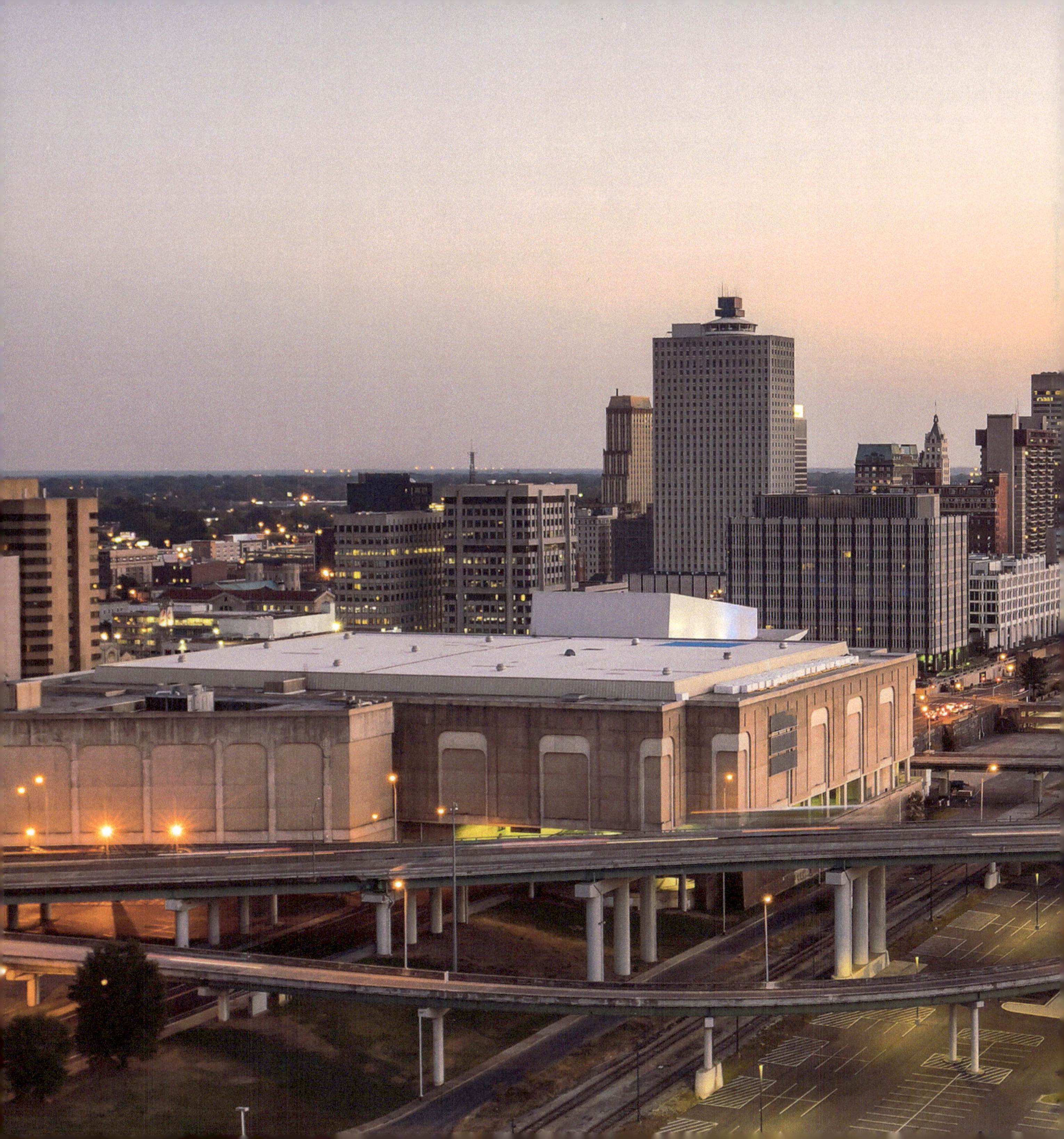

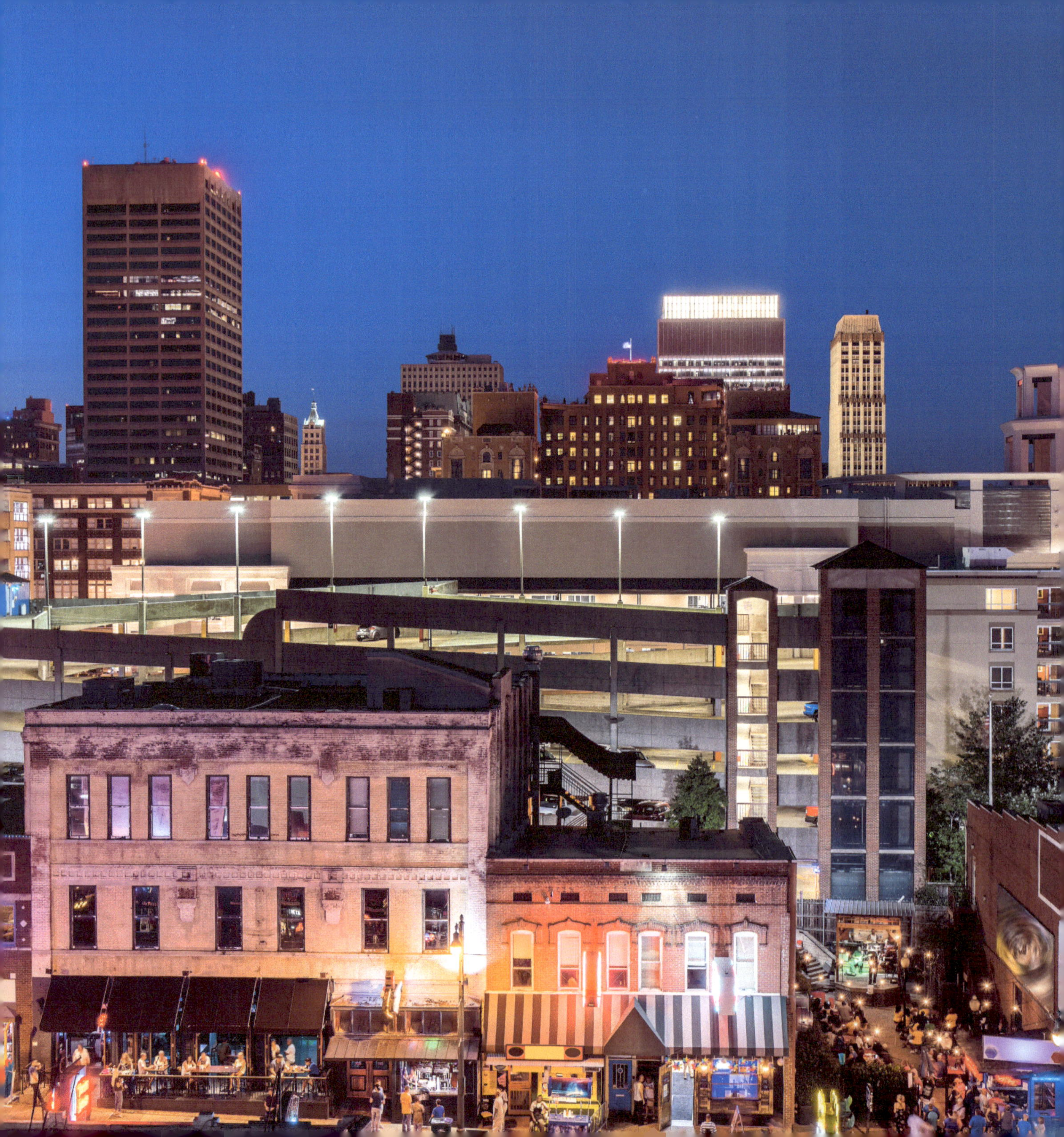

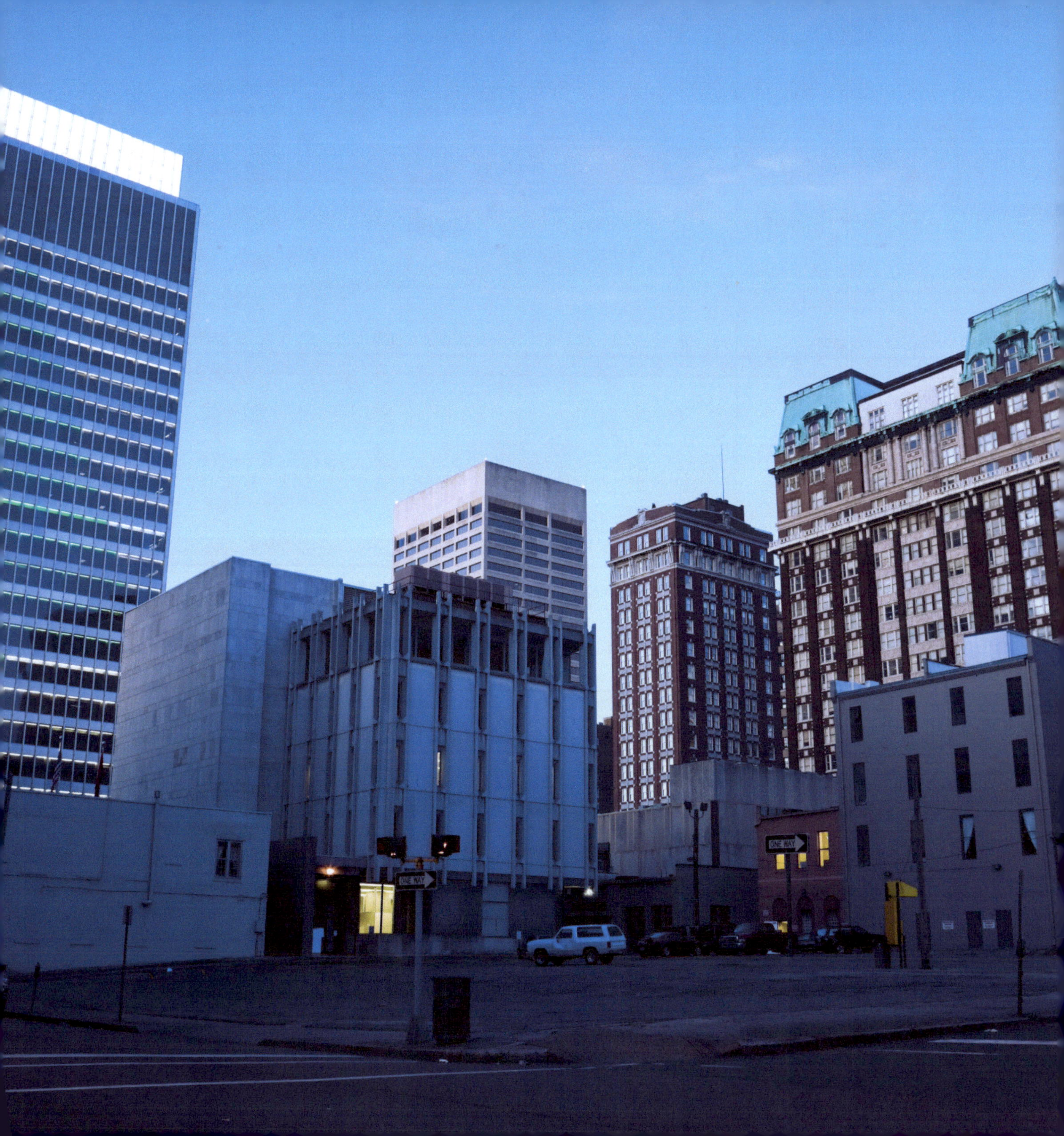
ONE WAY
ONE WAY

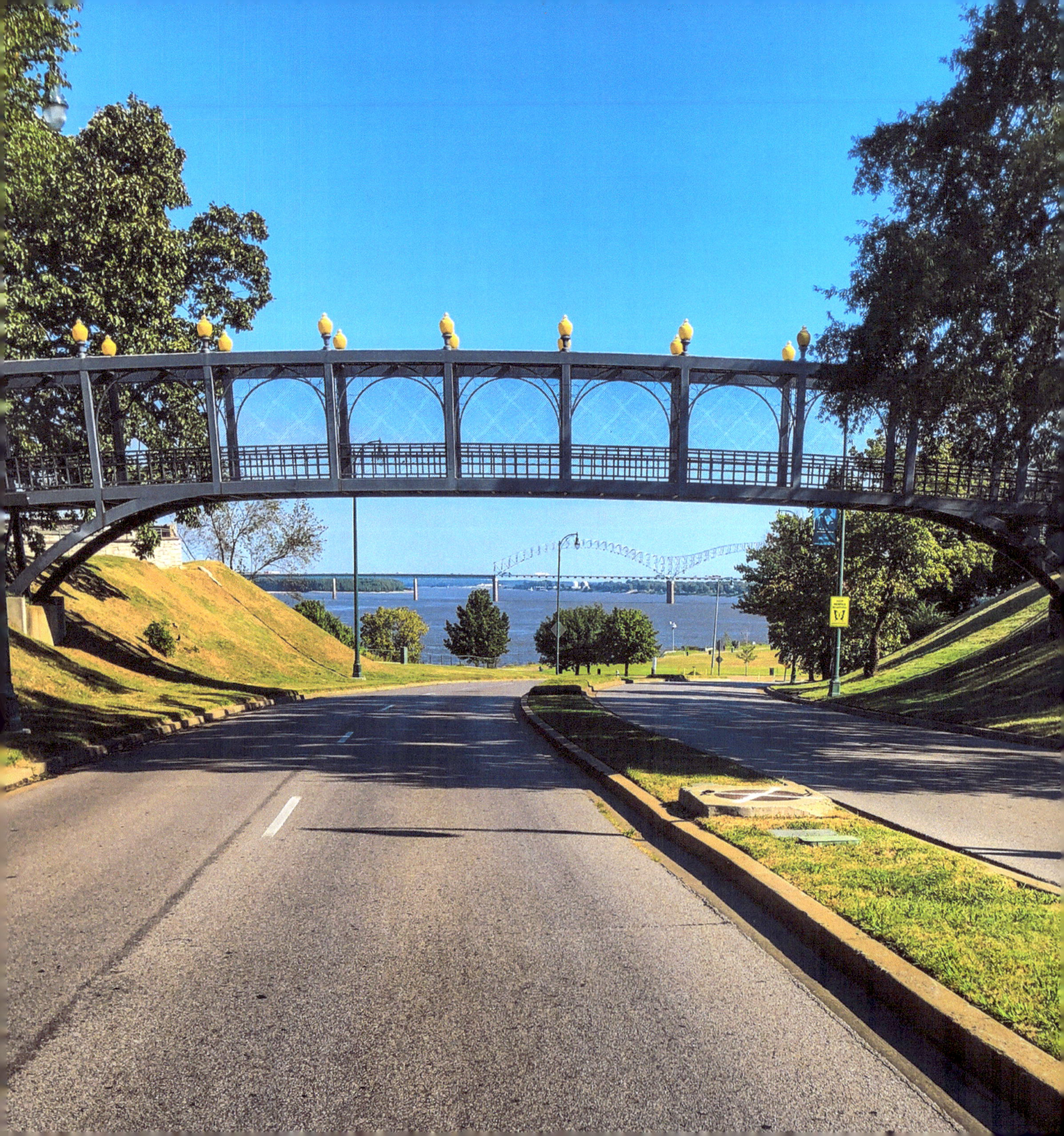

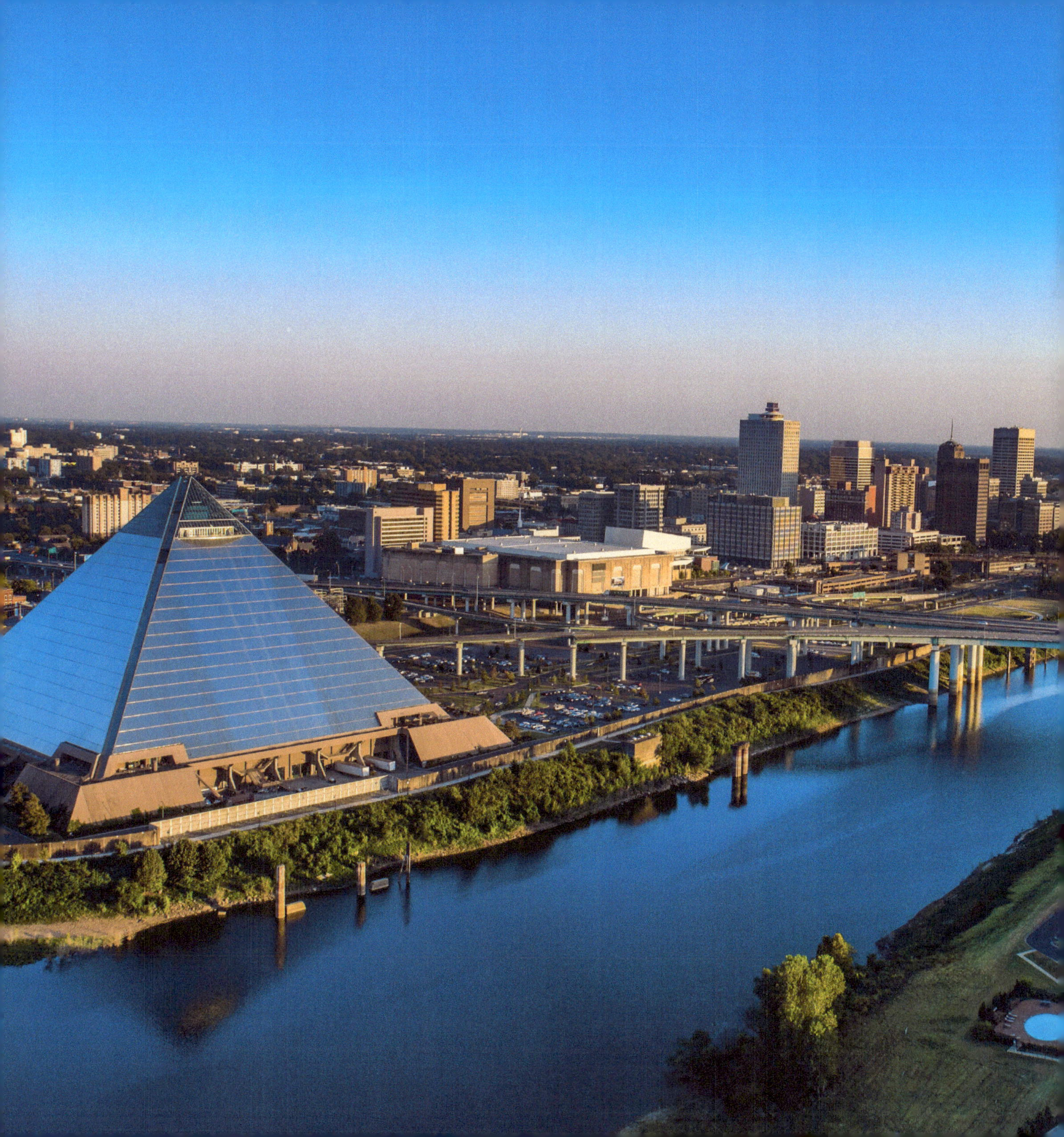

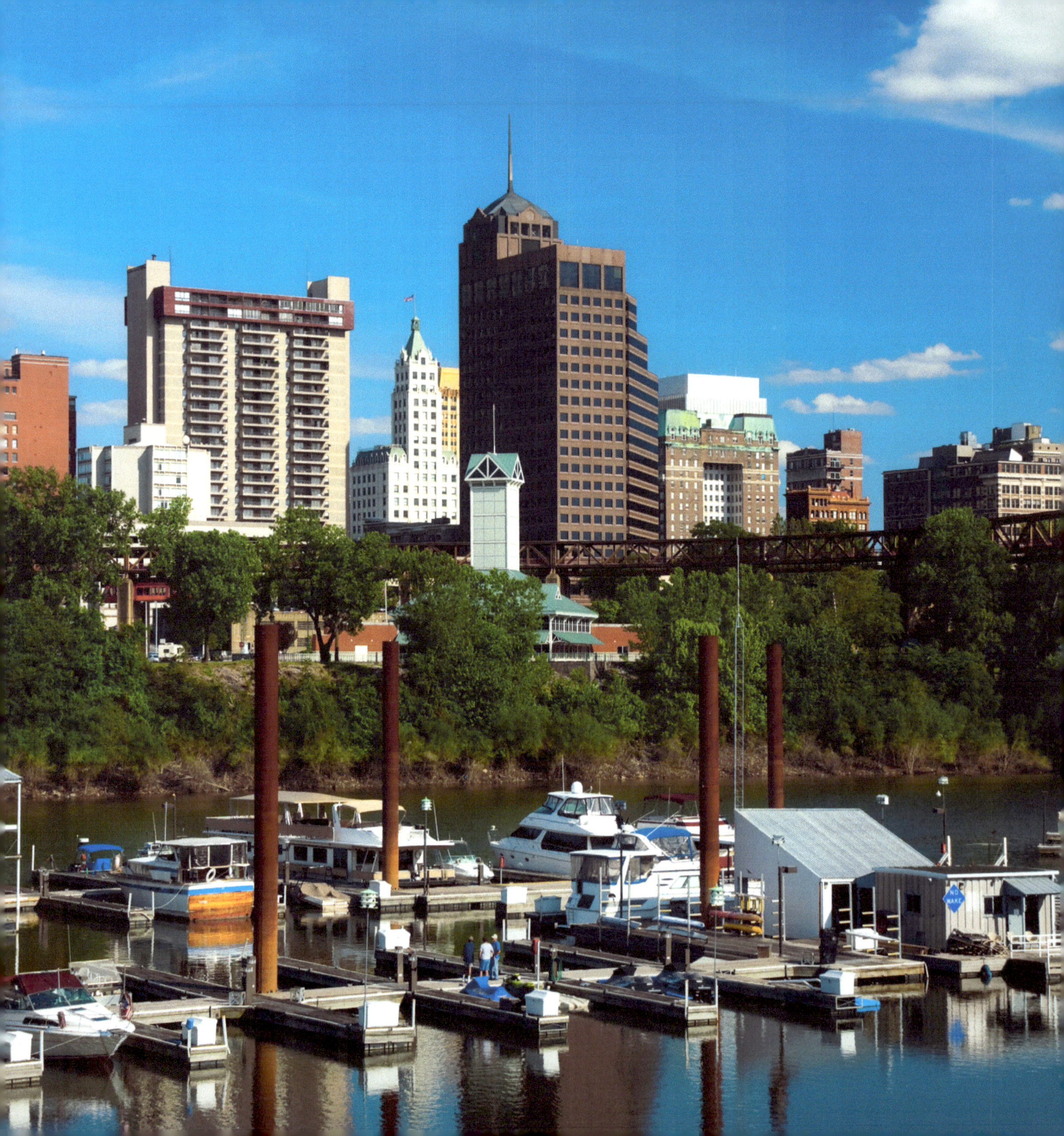
NO
WAKE

www.ingramcontent.com/pod-product-compliance
Lightning Source LLC
Chambersburg PA
CBHW040418220526
45473CB00004B/1275
* 9 7 9 8 4 2 3 2 6 8 8 9 3 *